With special thanks to our photographers

Sven Everaert
Bieke Claessens
Vincent Gyselinck
Els Prevenier

&

Paul Kusseneers
Concept & Lay-Out

&

Printed by De Plano

Compiled by: Lieve Cafmeyer
Concept & lay-out: Paul Kusseneers
Printed by: De Plano
Pre-press: Paul Kusseneers
Texts: Anne & Owen Davis
List of photographers:

Bieke Claessens : The Halcyon, Fountains, myhotel Bloomsbury, Belgo Zuid, Little Italy, Rules, St.Martins Lane, The Connaught, Quo Vadis, N° 5 Maddox Street.

Sven Everaert : Carluccio's, Caviar House, The Rookery, The Milestone Hotel & Appartments, Oxo Tower Restaurant, Bar & Brasserie, Momo Restaurant, The New Veeraswamy, Wok.Wok, Covent Garden Hotel, Clarke's, The Metropolitan, The Halkin, Harvey Nichols The Fifth Floor restaurant, Prism Restaurant & Bar, Bluebird Restaurant & Bar, Mirabelle, Yo! Sushi, l'Escargot, Rules, Sanderson, The Great Eastern Hotel, Assaggi, Livebait, Bibendum.

Vincent Gyselinck : The Cliveden Town House, One Aldwych, The Portobello Hotel, N° 11 Cadogan Gardens, Momo Restaurant, Sydney House, Quaglino's.

Els Prevenier : The Gastrodrome, Vong, Bentley's, Fish!, Julie's, Bank

ISBN 90-76124-28-0   D/2000/8101/5

First edition

LONDON Impressions

Hotels & Restaurants

Fountains Suites

COMPILED BY

LIEVE CAFMEYER

WRITTEN BY

ANNE & OWEN DAVIS

PUBLISHERS D-PUBLICATIONS

LONDON Impressions

London, the great and lively metropolis on the river Thames, was once the very centre of the greatest empire ever, influenced by many different cultures. In spite of that, the city has kept its own traditions as no other capital has.

Also, London is becoming more and more the trendsetter in the field of design. A trend which also is to be felt in the local restaurants and hotels.

This book is a voyage to typical hotels, where we discover both the London of Charles Dickens and discreet 19th—century mansions as well as hotels that are real temples of modern design.

On the culinary side, we travel around the world in restaurants with the finest of French and Italian cuisine. We savour eastern delicacies, from wok dishes to sushi, from Indian cuisine to Moroccan delights. And we have a wonderful taste of the new 'fusion' kitchen, served in the trendy Conran restaurants, with the Thames and the London skyline in the background.

We also savour the England of the twenties and thirties, in 'classics' such as Rules and Bentley's.

THE COLLECTION

THE COLLECTION

COVENT GARDEN HOTEL

Many hotel visitors are in the capital as theatre-goers. London's West End theatres are a magnet for visitors from across the world. It has perhaps always been an underlying theme of hotel life, however discreet, quietly restrained and traditional the presentation might be, that hotels themselves are places of theatre, too, with parts for each staff member and every guest. The restaurant, the bar, the corridors and rooms, but especially the lobby, are scene-setting locations for the dramatic unfolding of each new day. The Covent Garden district is conveniently close to West End theatreland and the Covent Garden Hotel stands centre stage in this popular and bustling area of London, full of designer shops, jugglers, chic restaurants like the Ivy, bearded stallholders, bookshops, fire-eaters and scores of innovative café-bars.

The Covent Garden Hotel has only 50 rooms and you might pass by its modest olive green entrance. The interior, though, is vivid and surprising, full of flavour and fun, yet still, oddly enough, solidly imbued with tradition - wood-panelling and portraits in oils on the walls, leather-bound tomes and paintings of gun dogs in the drawing-room and fabrics, embroideries and upholstery in Indian-like colour combinations of plum and turmeric.

The Covent Garden Hotel is a town house in the Knightsbridge and Chelsea style. It may be small, but it is hugely popular with media and entertainment figures. It may be no coincidence that a recent expansion includes a 50-seat state-of-the-art cinema with two adjacent reception rooms, available for special hire or for screening current films for the pleasure of the hotel's guests. Owners Tim and Kit Kemp have created one of the very best-appointed little hotels to be found anywhere. Its lively lobby houses the Brasserie Max, a convenient place to sit down to a tasty meal before setting off for a play or a musical. A stone stairway leads up to the superb library on the one hand and the elegant drawing-room on the other, where most evenings of the year a cosy log fire crackles. While you're in there, seek out the exquisite antique marquetry writing-desk - it will take your breath away.

The rooms are no less than perfect, each has a luxurious bathroom suite, a VCR, two-line phone, fax and modem, a safe and a large antique desk of its own. The Loft Suite is the most special of all. It is situated, as its name would suggest, at the top of the house, on two floors, with tall ceilings and a gallery-style bedroom.

It's time, I suggest, to star in your own play. There'll be no critics to praise or damn your performance as you stroll across the lobby to sign in at the reception desk of the Covent Garden Hotel - but you'll certainly be well received and carry off with you when you leave a bouquet of happy memories.

THE METROPOLITAN

The Metropolitan could hardly be more central. It is the first new hotel to open in prestigious Park Lane for over twenty years. Hyde Park, Mayfair, Bond Street and the West End… you can walk to them all in moments. But in spite of its location, right in the very heart of London, the hotel is wonderfully peaceful.

Perhaps it is the contemporary simplicity of the design - hardwoods, marbles and printed, natural fabrics are used boldly and unadorned, with all non-essentials stripped away. Perhaps the extremely effective acoustic double-glazing throughout contributes not a little to the all-pervading sense of Zen-like quietude.

The Japanese allusion is apt. The exquisite Penthouse Suite, jewel in The Metropolitan's crown, is encircled by a stone garden that would be at home in a Kyoto monastery. And the hotel's partner venture, the Nobu restaurant, which occupies the entire first floor, is renowned for its modern and innovative Japanese cuisine.

The celebrated chef Nobuyuki Matsuhisa, who has other restaurants in Los Angeles, New York and Tokyo, trained as a sushi chef and then travelled extensively, particularly in South America and interesting, original influences from that country can be found in the marvellously succesful menu at Nobu. The restaurant, which also has a sushi bar, opened in 1997 and was awarded a Michelin star in 1998 and again in 1999.
Also located at the Metropolitan is the stylish and lively Met Bar. In the short time it has been open, the Met Bar has become one of the *happening* meeting places on the fashionable London scene and is certainly where to be if you're a martini cocktail fan. There are no less than 26 different martinis on the menu, and dozens more available 'off-menu'… just ask!

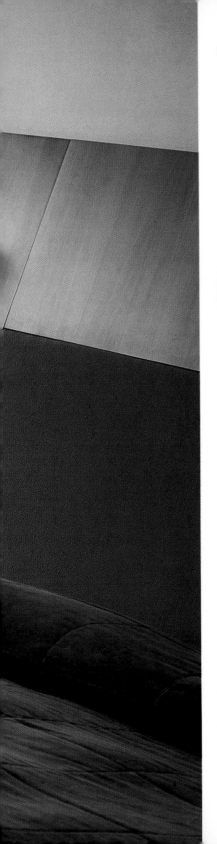

The Met Bar is open all day, even for an early breakfast, but after 6 p.m. it is only open to members and to the Metropolitan's residents.

The 18 suites and 155 guest rooms at the Metropolitan have an extensive list of top-of-the-range business facilities, including ISDN line, voice mail, modem and fax - and secretarial services are available at short notice.

If you've had a tense and busy day of meetings and phone calls, head for the gym and treatment suites: a range of relaxing massages and therapies is available, including shiatsu, reflexology and aromatherapy. Throughout this tranquil and luxurious hotel you are surrounded by gorgeous and often surprisingly fresh design features - carpets like abstract paintings by Helen Yardley, curved glass coffee tables, deep pastel-shaded sofas… and lots of natural light flowing in through huge windows. Even your porter will be dressed by Donna Karan. Discreet, severe and sophisticated - that's the Metropolitan.

THE CONNAUGHT HOTEL

The evening before I stepped through the portals of the Connaught Hotel into the magnificent mahogany-panelled lobby, I had dined at Rules, that most traditionally English of restaurants, and immediately I sensed a kindred feeling in the air here, a warm and restrained elegance, a dignified affection for the old values of courteous, even courtly, service, the very highest standards of comfort and good taste.

The Connaught, situated in a peaceful residential area of Mayfair, was originally created as a refuge for the landed gentry during their forays into the capital. It opened in 1897 to immediate acclaim and to this day has retained its classic poise, its atmosphere of a refined country house, and its popularity.

There are many who would consider the Connaught their London residence, who return time and again and find to their satisfaction that the same familiar faces are there to care for them still.

I mounted the grand gleaming mahogany staircase to my first-floor room with a feeling of deep pleasure and anticipation. Fresh flowers awaited me, thick curtains reached to the floor, an elegant chandelier twinkled with a hundred points of light. At the touch of a button, I might summon my own butler; one is assigned to each floor.

Sadly, I could not imagine a thing that I required of him. There was a marble bathroom, where a fluffy bathrobe and a snug pair of slippers awaited me.

After a long and luxurious soak, I took myself down to the oak-panelled cocktail bar for a drink. Even the bar - quiet, relaxed and intimate - has won itself an award.

The restaurant at the Connaught is Michelin-starred. Head chef Michel Bourdin is highly regarded for his mastery, both of traditional English dishes and classic French cuisine. I might have chosen from the *grande carte*, but to remain in keeping with my surroundings, I chose a steak and kidney pudding with fresh vegetables, a plain enough dish, but given Michel's touch it was more special than any pie I had eaten before.

The glittering main restaurant has 75 covers, but for a more private occasion there is the Grill Room or even the beautiful Regency Carlos Suite, which has an adjacent conservatory for aperitifs.

After my meal I took coffee in one of the lounges and as it was a balmy late summer evening, I went for a leisurely stroll round nearby Berkeley Square. I thought of the landed gentry of yesteryear, who came here to visit a very different London, and was grateful that in a rapidly changing world, some good things remain the same - the Connaught, for instance.

SYDNEY HOUSE

Chelsea is London at its best. On Sloane Square, well-dressed young ladies step out of taxis, their hands full of shopping bags with discreet designer logos. In King's Road, elegant shops display the very best of antiques and interior design, the latest fashions. Those who live here have taste and class, those who shop here have an eye for what is different. The houses have a long, fascinating history, the restaurants in the area serve the best from across the world. And if you would like to stay here in gracious style, reserve a room at Sydney House.

Everything about Sydney House exudes peace and elegance. The beautifully restored nineteenth-century building has high and stately windows with wrought-iron balconies. Inside, everything is impregnated with the glamour that only real *understated chic* can offer. Fashion designers, photographers and models have made this their second home, international companies who want to pamper their executives, book rooms here for their foreign business associates.

The 23 rooms are each different and each special. In the Tiger room, the bedspread seems to have been recently shot by a big game hunter; in the Royal Room, privileged guests sleep in a gilded four-poster bed draped in silks and brocades. Each room leads you into a different world, from Indonesia to Paris.

Designer-hotelier Jean-Luc Aeby is from Switzerland and clearly has an eye for the kind of antiques that are quirky and beautiful. In the lobby with its rich carpets, gilt mirrors and a wonderful crystal chandelier stands a bust of the Venus de Milo, whom he calls the symbol of Sydney House. Vibrant colours, luxurious materials and carefully chosen works of art make the hotel a wonderful temporary home.

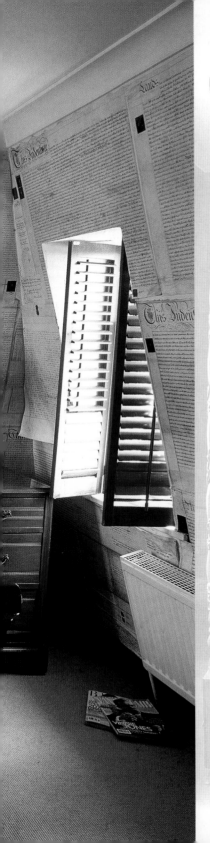

The restaurant serves only breakfast and light meals… but that is all that is required. After all, Chelsea has so much to offer that it would be a shame not to venture out and find a restaurant to your taste. Jean-Luc Aeby is more that pre-pared to tell you where to go and -just as important- which places to avoid. And if, back in the lobby of Sydney House, you see a face that you recog-nise from the cover of Vogue, you look away discreetly. For this is a house where people want to feel at home.

THE HALKIN

Behind a courtly Georgian façade in a quiet street in London's fashionable Belgravia, only a short walk from Knightsbridge, you will find one of the capital's most contemporary, high-tech and sophisticated hotels.

The post-modern Halkin, despite its English name, is Italian to its very heart. It was created and is owned by Christina Ong, and was designed by Laboratorio Associati, studio of the Milanese team of Lorenzo Carmellini and Rocco Magnoli. The white uniforms worn by the hotel staff were designed by none less than Giorgio Armani, and the Michelin-starred restaurant, named after its head chef, Stefano Cavallini, offers an individual and modern Milanese cuisine, devised and honed to perfection by Stefan and his talented team.

The Halkin was named Egon Ronay Hotel of the Year in 1995, just four years after the hotel first opened, and has already won a clutch of other prestigious awards. From the moment you step through its portals onto the lobby's polished marble floors, it is easy to see why.

Each floor has been designed around a colour signifying earth, air, fire and water. Gracefully curved corridors lead to rooms and suites that have a minimalist feel, but are not severe at all - perhaps because they benefit from the advice of a Feng Shui consultant. Grey, black and cream furnishings and fabrics are complemented by warm rosewood panelling and sophisticated lighting. As soon as you insert your electronic tag and open your door, lights flick on and your room comes comfortably to life.

The beds are fitted with Egyptian cotton sheets and goosedown pillows, and each bathroom is constructed of marble, with deep baths, thick towels and complimentary Bvlgari toiletries. The traveller visiting London will find it difficult to decide how to spend his days, there is so much for him to choose from. The business guest, too, will have a long and busy schedule… but as evening descends, the Cavallini Restaurant with its sleek, contemporary interior is a great place to wind down and enjoy a satisfying meal. Specialities include stuffed gnocchi with artichokes, served with white wine and ginger sauce, or partridge with pomegranate, turnip and celeriac purée. There is a distinguished list of Italian wines.

The Halkin is a refuge for the connoisseur and a delight on every count.

ELEVEN CADOGAN GARDENS

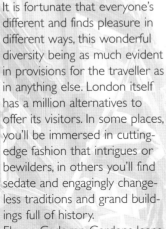

It is fortunate that everyone's different and finds pleasure in different ways, this wonderful diversity being as much evident in provisions for the traveller as in anything else. London itself has a million alternatives to offer its visitors. In some places, you'll be immersed in cutting-edge fashion that intrigues or bewilders, in others you'll find sedate and engagingly change-less traditions and grand build-ings full of history.

Eleven Cadogan Gardens leans more to the latter. In a quiet, tree-lined square off the main thoroughfare of Knightsbridge, a few short paces from Sloane Street and fashionable Kings Road, stands an elegant town house that was one of the first, in 1949, to open its doors as an hotel for the discerning. In fact, the premises have since swallowed up three of its fel-lows, to reach its present size. With oak-panelled rooms hung with oil paintings and furnished with fine antiques and oriental rugs, it has that warmly tradi-tional feel that, I fervently hope, will never go out of fashion. There is nothing outside except a discreet Number 11 to identify this very special building, yet every taxidriver will be able to deliver you to the door without much ado. From the moment the front door opens for you and a porter relieves you of your bags, it's as if you were visiting friends in the capital. Personal care is such that you might imagine a butler all your own were at your beck and call. Many guests return time and again and count the long-ser-ving and devoted staff as friends. If you so desire a chauffeured Mercedes is at your disposal.

At present, wonderful English breakfasts will be brought to your room, and light meals are available 24 hours a day, which can be served either in your room or in the drawing-room, but soon, a light-filled, airy dining room will be. It has been built on the ground floor around two small courtyards. It will have a warm and welcoming fireplace where newly-arrived guests can relax and savour their environment. A Portland stone floor with oak strips and light-painted panelling add to the friendly atmosphere, and the food will be wholesome and organic as far as reasonably possible. After a long day exploring London, I sat in a wing chair with an Armagnac in my hand… and dreamed. Dreams can indeed come true: a stay at Eleven Cadogan Gardens is proof of that.

It will drop you off for an appointment with a business colleague, perhaps, at a major auction house, even help with a trip to the shops, a museum or the theatre… and finally, at the end of your stay, transport you in restful luxury back to the airport.

There are 60 luxurious rooms altogether, each individually furnished, and many of them overlook the private Cadogan Gardens themselves, which guests are free to use whenever they wish.

FOUNTAINS SUITES

Hyde Park in spring. On a bench, a girl spoons yoghurt out of a pot. She has left the company canteen and has come here to feel the first rays of sunshine. Speaker's Corner is quiet; the weather is too nice to campaign against anything. In the Italian Water Gardens, a young couple have eyes only for each other. Sunlight slants through open doors on the second floor of Fountains, falls on the chaise longue near the balcony. Sometimes, city life can be like a holiday.

Many lovers of England dream of an apartment in London, in one of those vibrant neighbourhoods that make the capital so special. Travellers who'd like to know, however briefly, what it's like to be a Londoner, can now fulfil their dreams.

In Hyde Park stands a discreet art deco building that has lost none of its original charm. Just as charming are the 16 apartments within, every single one a prime example of timeless elegance and contemporary luxury. With one or even several bedrooms, for a weekend for two or up to seven people, Fountains is a home away from home.

The best in British design has been brought together: great names like furniture designer Mark Brazier-Jones and interior designer Christopher Nevile have given Fountains their personal touch. Fountains Suites is a unique concept that offers all the privacy of a home, all the service of the best hotels.

If you wish, you can experiment with the many flavours of London, do your own food shopping, and prepare your own meal in your state-of-the-art kitchen. Or you can take advantage of 24-hour room service. Even entertaining is made easy: a chef and butler can come to prepare and serve a gourmet meal in your apartment. And then there is London. With every kind of entertainment, restaurants and theatres, shopping streets and historical buildings within walking distance. And Hyde Park, with the Water Gardens as your front yard. To be a Londoner for a weekend or a week - a suite at Fountains will make the experience unforgettable.

N° 5 MADDOX STREET

Five o'clock in London. Commuters hurry towards the Underground which will take them to Waterloo Station, where their train to the suburbs waits. In the Museum of the Moving Image a young guide discreetly yawns behind his hand. The pubs fill up with office workers and labourers, secretaries and ladies of leisure arriving for a drink at the end of a long day. In Chinatown, a restaurant chef chops vegetables for the wok… for him, the day is just beginning.

Number 5, Maddox Street, is like an oasis of peace. In the trendy West End, between the shopping areas of Bond Street and Regent Street, a small, quiet street hides, where you can almost forget the busy city is so close by. This is home to 12 luxurious suites with one, two or three bedrooms, each with its own kitchen, where weary travellers or excited tourists can find a little peace and quiet, a perfect antidote to the busy London life outside. The interiors are a relaxing and clever combination of east and west.

The comfortable, clean-lined furniture has organic colours: browns and beiges, terracottas, stone greys, inky blues… Glass, metal and tactile materials are used in perfect harmony. On a bed lies a throw of faux sabre, a touch of luxury against a stylish background. Aroma stones and therapeutic oils add to the relaxing feeling. The bamboo floors are so shiny that the dancing flames of the open fire are reflected in it. And on the private terrace, bamboo furniture, pebbles and green plants create an atmosphere of serenity. Seven o'clock in London. Early diners sip pre-dinner drinks and examine the restaurant menu. The theatres get ready to open their doors, in front of the cinemas with all the latest films, queues begin to form. And the suite at N° 5 Maddox Street, with a warm glowing fire, is so peaceful that dinner is postponed for a while. You open the patio doors and breathe in the cool London air. And make plans for later that evening, for the night is still young.

HALCYON HOTEL

Kensington, Mayfair, Chelsea - districts such as these are recognised world-wide as London's most fashionable, chock-full of great hotels, shops of distinction and celebrated restaurants. Notting Hill, since the eponymous film starring Hugh Grant and Julia Roberts was released to such acclaim, is not lagging far behind. Just down the road from there is elegant Holland Park, fast becoming a name with a cachet as desirable as any location in the capital.

Not more than a short walk from the BBC studios in Shepherd's Bush, and within easy reach of Knightsbridge, home of Harrods, and a brief taxi ride from Oxford Street, Bond Street, Piccadilly and all the shops, museums, theatres and buzzing night-life of central London and picturesque Soho, the discreet and quietly imposing streets of Holland Park offer stylish refuge.

As the name suggests, there is indeed a park here, leafy and idyllic, around which the classic white-painted villas are gathered. Here, in this favoured spot, you will find one of London's best small hotels, the Halcyon. Two grand Belle Epoque stucco town houses have been meticulously restored to blend seamlessly with the imposing ambassador-ial residences that surround it. Some rooms offer traditional four-poster beds, others have a jacuzzi or maybe a wonderful tented ceiling. You'll find a Russian room, a romantic Mughal room, even a stunning Egyptian room, nestling up under the eaves. French windows open invitingly onto ivy-wound balconies.

From the moment you step through the door into the impressive reception area where in the cooler months a log fire crackles merrily and an elderly but imposing grandfather clock stands guard, you are embraced by the utmost luxury, courtesy and discretion. But there is more. The Halcyon possesses a stylish and friendly cocktail bar, and a restaurant, called simply The Room, that has built itself a reputation as one of the very best in town. 'Exciting, mouth-watering dishes' Egon Ronay has enthused, and other publications have followed with equally generous applause.

Head chef Martin Hadden has only recently handed over his mantle to Toby Hill, youngest-ever winner of a Michelin star, who describes his dishes as 'light, seasonal and contemporary'. In fine weather, guests can eat outside on the Provençal-style garden terrace, which is enclosed, like a choice secret, within high protective walls. The Halcyon is atmospheric, imaginative and discreet - just the sort of exclusive hideaway celebrities would seek out, and indeed they seem to have made the hotel their own. Altogether an unforgettable experience - even if no famous personage crosses your path at all.

MY HOTEL BLOOMSBURY

Bloomsbury is one of my favourite areas of London, very central and yet preserving a sense of quietude. Patrician townhouses stand on all four sides of Bedford Square, with a leafy, friendly park in the middle.

In Bayley Street, just off Bedford Square, and on the site of the old Bedford Corner Hotel, an hotel has opened its doors that promises, like the new St. Martins Lane Hotel in Covent Garden, a new vision of customer care… an hotel for the Millennium.

Styled as a contemporary interpretation of the graceful old townhouses that surround it, myhotel bloomsbury, with 76 rooms and a philosophy behind each one of them, is the first in what is to be a brand chain in the decades ahead, a venture full of optimism and spirituality. Andy Thrasyvoulou has chosen two design gurus to help him realise his dream: Terence Conran, by way of his architecture and design company,

Conran Design, and American master of *feng shui* William Spear.

What they have come up with is a very new and fairly minimal hotel, with clean lines and cool lineny colours, some splashes of mostly blues or orange in the fabrics, and plenty of light wood, airy and uncluttered. A sparse environment, but with touches of obvious luxury.

There's mybar, for a start, where I checked in, sitting comfortably with a drink in hand, rather than propped at the reception desk. And there's mypreferences, a sheet I'd received two weeks earlier, inviting me to share my likes and wishes - I found my favourite Early English keyboard music ready beside the CD player.

Mychi is the hotel's restaurant, which is open all day long and serves very fresh, light, healthy dishes from both East and West, just another way this unusual hotel blends complementary cultures to the benefit of its guests.

I was impressed with the curried fish I ordered with side dishes of vegetables and a fragrant bowl of saffron rice… all most attractively presented. Whether the yin balanced the yang, I'm not qualified to report. All I can say is that the food sat very lightly on my stomach and I felt a happy contentment, which is precisely the aim of myhotel.

If I'd had a business conference to attend, myhotel would be my choice… they have gone to endless trouble, down to the smallest detail, to provide the friendliest and most relaxing of spaces for meetings, conferences and private dining. Altogether, a young and very cool up-to-the-minute hotel that truly is different, that takes good health and a calm mind seriously, that takes the concept of service a step beyond. Things are happening in London, and myhotel is among the best of them.

CLIVEDEN TOWN HOUSE

The palatial and historic Cliveden Hotel, once the country home of the Astors, is a magnificent landmark on the banks of the Thames in Berkshire and is widely regarded as one of the top hotels in Britain. Now the same high levels of personal attention and luxury are available right in the heart of London.

The Cliveden Town House is an extension of that fine hotel. It stands on a quiet square overlooking lovely gardens full of cherry-trees and bird song, but is only a conveniently short walk from Harrods and fashionable Kensington High Street; the West End theatres are hardly much further away. Nancy Astor's grandson William, fourth Viscount Astor, is on the board of the Cliveden Hotel. He has said 'It seemed a pity for our guests to be dropped off at a London hotel that, however luxurious, would always be impersonal by comparison.' And so the concept of a London 'outpost' of the grand country residence was conceived... and carried through to a triumphant conclusion by designers Rupert Lord and Carole Roberts, both of whom had worked on the Cliveden Hotel.

Two late 19th century houses, tucked discreetly behind trendy Sloane Square in Cadogan Gardens, were found and painstakingly restored.
The same grand yet characteristically informal style guests enjoy at the Cliveden Hotel can be found throughout the Town House. Each private space has been designed quite differently, yet within an overal theatrical theme. They are decorated with carefully chosen and

cleverly-placed *objets d'art*, which look as if they were borrowed from forgotten bedrooms in some rambling old wisteria-hung family mansion. The bedrooms are spacious, light-ceilinged and gracefully proportioned, their walls hung with original portraits, fascinating prints and mementoes. Often they relate to famous men and women of the theatre, after whom all the rooms are named.

An excellent room service is available 24 hours a day, and it can be a pleasure to eat an intimate supper before your own fire. But in the morning, I'd recommend you step downstairs and enjoy the friendly atmosphere in the Breakfast Room.

The public rooms, which include a comfortable library and a peaceful drawing-room that looks out onto the gardens, are gracious yet homely, set about with comfortable chairs and deep sofas, open fires crackling in the grates, newspapers and magazines laid out on elegant antique tables, pots of afternoon tea steaming cosily before tired new arrivals. At the Cliveden Town House, the unspoken motto is 'make yourself at home'.

ONE ALDWYCH

Outside, it's a tall, graceful, decorative Edwardian structure in granite curved around a busy junction of the Aldwych and the Strand, with a green copper cupola and a stone balustrade. Inside, it's contemporary, cool and utterly stylish. Design flair is evident, from the overall welcoming feel of the vast lobby, through each and every corridor, to the minutiae of the 105 guest rooms. The aesthetics of One Aldwych,

constitute, to my mind, a modern classic of unerring taste, yet visually surprising and exciting. Within six months of its opening in July 1998, the five-star hotel has won two major international design awards, and has been voted AA Hotel of the Year 2000.

Hard to imagine that its origins were so workmanlike: the building originally housed The Morning Post, a newspaper now long defunct, but clearly not without aspirations of grandeur in its day.

The hotel lobby has retained many of the features from the paper's heyday - dramatically tall windows, columns and oak pannelling. All else has been pared away and then deliciously reworked.

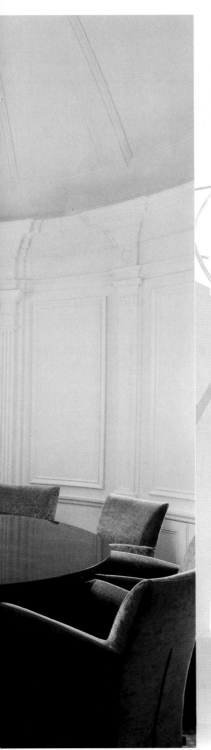

Owner and Managing Director Gordon Campbell Gray's vision has been seeamlessly blended with the innovative skills of British designer Mary Fox Linton.

The 62-seat Indigo is One Aldwych's flagship restaurant. Set on the mezzanine, overlooking the dramatic double-height lobby, its decor is striking and the menu is full of exciting choices, offering a clever blend of eastern and western - beef, for instance, served with lobster and sweet vegetable roll with a Thai lime dressing. Executive chef is Julian Jenkins, who is responsible tor the Indigo, all room service and the hotel's three private dining suites, one of which is attached to the super-comfortable 30-seat screening room.

A second choice of restaurant is available. Axis is separately managed, has its own entrance and an entirely different kitchen, chef and menu. Its design is reminiscent of the 1920s and 30s. Head chef Mark Gregory is already something of a television personality and the author of two fascinating cook books. Axis, being so

close to a score of West End theatres, offers an express menu, in addition to its regular one, specifically to favour businessmen and theatre-goers who are short of time.

And then there is the Cinnamon Bar, which has an entrance of its own and which serves delicious soups, salads, sandwiches and pastries, as well as a range of healthy juices and shakes.

Cool jazz is dispensed from the sound system. But if you'd prefer another style of music, you could dive into the great 18-metre hotel pool and listen to some underwater Mozart!

Gordon Campbell Gray has said of this utterly delightful hotel: "I wanted it to have gravitas, while at the same time to feel truly modern, individual and exciting." He has realised his aims triumphantly, for One Aldwych is all that, but has not overlooked in its pursuit of visual excellence that - to quote its own motto - an hotel is 'ultimately, all about service'.

THE PORTOBELLO HOTEL

What makes a hotel into a legend? The special furnishings? The famous guests who have stayed there? The fickleness of a trendy public, which suddenly makes a certain address 'the place to be'? The Portobello Hotel, in Kensington, has a touch of all those things. It was opened in 1971, and right from the start it was special. Behind the walls of two Victorian houses overlooking a quiet garden, a very special world can be found.

The hotel has a timeless charm with a Victorian touch which has, in this *fin de siècle* era, become very much in demand. The very first guest was Richard Branson, and where he went, many well-known people followed. Tina Turner liked the hotel so much she bought the house next door. Alice Cooper slept there in a round bed that was bought especially for him. His pet python occupied the bath and they stayed for a month. Van Morrison wrote some of his songs here. And once, a couple bathed in champagne - it is said they were Kate Moss and Johnny Depp.

The Portobello is what is called a 'boutique' hotel. It is situated in the heart of London, adjacent to the famous Portobello Antique Market and close to the West End shops and theatres. Each of the twenty-four rooms is different, furnished in a bohemian mix of Victorian elements and eastern delights from the Arabian Nights. It gives the hotel a unique and unforgettable character. There is a honeymoon suite containing a four-poster bed which used to belong to Queen Victoria, which is so high that you need steps to climb into it. There is a room like a cosy ship's cabin. And, of course, there is the famous room with the round bed… and 100 year old bathing machine, complete with copper pipes and old-fashioned taps that can provide anything from gentle showers to real waves.

What makes a stay at The Portobello so unique, is the atmosphere of luxury mixed with a happy touch of decadence, of peace and quiet in the heart of a busy city. After a long day's shopping and sightseeing it's good to come home to a place where everything conspires to relax you.

The Portobello is an oasis, a legend and, most of all: an adventure.

THE ROOKERY

The City would seem to be a rather vague term, but in London it defines a very specific area of the capital - the 'Square mile' of the financial district. Here, in this busy maze of streets, a mile or two east of the centre of London, you'll find not only the headquarters of major banks and financial houses, but some of London's

best-known landmarks: P.C. Wren's domed masterpiece St. Paul's Cathedral; the Old Bailey, the venerable crimininal court where many major trials are still conducted today, the Guildhall, and the excitingly contemporary and ever-lively Barbican Arts Centre. Historically, this area managed also the be bohemian and raffish, a sort of Soho outside Soho, but with a rather more villainous reputation. It is here, supposedly, that Fagan, Charles Dickens' immortal baddie, plied his dark trade.

Those days are gone, but Clerkenwell, home of Smithfield Meat market and the colourful Asian communities around Brick Lane, still boasts an exuberant street life.

Here you will find a gem of a small hotel. Called, with restrained and charming modesty, The Rookery, it is the most recent venture of Peter McKay and Douglas Blair, the pair behind two other of London's best establishments: the Gore, in Kensington and Hazlitt's, in Soho.

They spent three years painstakingly refurbishing a row of 18th century brick buildings in tree-shaded Cowcross Street, and then furnishing it with great care and superior taste to create an hotel of immense period charm, with extensive wood panelling, flag-stone floors, cheerful open fires and wonderfully chosen antiques and paintings, some of which come from their own private collection.

Each of its 33 comfortable and homely bedrooms is different, named after actual residents who lived here over a century ago. The very best of these is the Rook's Nest, indeed like an eyrie, set high up amidst the rafters and fashioned on two levels, with a spire and incredible views across the rooftops to St. Paul's. There is even space in the sumptuous bedroom for a real Edwardian bathing-machine!

Tucked away in its little oasis of calm, this is an enchanting place, with the subdued and intimate air of a gentleman's club. It is hard to believe that it can be found in the heart of a City bustling with activity.

ST MARTINS LANE

Ian Schrager has always been a figure at the cutting-edge of innovative popular culture. Just remember New York's Studio 5A; in the '70s it was the club for the celebrities and wild things of the day and it was opened by Schrager and Steve Rubell.

Today he is still thinking ahead of the pack. He has shifted his sights across the Atlantic from his native America and recently opened not one but two ground-breaking concept hotels in London, the St Martins Lane and, in Soho, the equally stunning Sanderson Hotel. His appealing idea of 'hotel as theatre' has met with tremendous success in Miami, New York and Los Angeles and at the new St. Martins Lane Hotel, in Covent Garden, Europeans can now experience his exciting concepts on their own doorstep. One might not imagine there is much to be done in the way of innovation when offering room and board, but that would be reckoning without the invention of a man of vision. St Martins Lane should not be thought as an an hotel but as an 'urban resort', where guests, according to Schrager, will discover an experience that is magical and unforgettable.

So what makes this hotel so special? Ian Schrager turned, once more, to idiosyncratic design guru Philippe Starck, whose stamp can be found in the grand vistas and in little particulars, from the improbably tall, luminescent yellow glass revolving doors that allow you into the lobby to the shape of the bath in your private rooms.

Let's begin in the lobby. It is a truly magnificent spectacle, awash with light, activity and colour. It is soaring and theatrical, a huge space, a gathering of six restaurants and bars, overseen by a single head chef or director, Jeffery Chodoron, already an internationally celebrated restaurateur.

There is the Asia de Cuba, with its stunning and majestic 'art columns' and wonderfully creative Asian-Latino fare, the Saint M, a thoroughly modern interpretation of the Parisian brasserie and the Sea Bar, serving perfect sushi and every kind of seafood, a theatrical extravaganza, with mounds of glowing ice and a bewitching wall of bubbles.

And there's the Rum Bar, too, and a gorgeously landscaped Sidewalk Café and, taking you right outdoors, the Outdoor Garden Restaurant.

Starck's approach is if not exactly minimalist, then at least simple, under- rather than over-decorated, and is, as a result, serene and practical, supremely comfortable and infinitely stylish.

All this is evident in the 204 guest rooms, which have one amazing feature in common - an interactive light installation that lets each guest choose his own dramatic lighting programme. Viewed from the street, the personalised rooms turn the hotel's façade into a captivating mosaic of light. When you book into St Martins Lane, you don't just buy a room for the night, you buy into a magical 21st century experience that you will not soon forget.

THE MILESTONE HOTEL & APARTMENTS

Opulence is not a word I would use very often, but it cannot be avoided in a description of this magnificent hotel, that draws together two gracious 19th century town houses with uninterrupted views across trees and parkland to the famous Kensington Palace, home of the late Princess Diana.

A no-expenses-spared refurbishment of the Milestone Hotel & Apartments has left intact as many period details and original architectural features as possible, both inside and out.

The atmosphere of the Milestone is that of nothing less than a stately home. The warm and benign patina of history and privilege envelops you from the moment you step into the lobby. You can choose a room, a suite, or go one step further still and take a whole two or three bedroom apartment, all of them richly furnished with the utmost of good taste.

This wealth of luxurious appointments is only the beginning of the Milestone story. Service, too, is of the very best. I was offered - it was my own choice - a pot of relaxing green tea upon my arrival or I might have taken a sherry or a celebratory glass of champagne.

In the early evening, a butler arrived at my door to 'turn down' - a process which included placing a hot water bottle in the bed, a fresh bottle of mineral water on the antique table, together with a plate of delicious canapés and then a conscientious survey of my vase of flowers and the fruit bowl, switching on the bedside booklights and touching a flame to a pair of floating candles. The convenience of a butler service continues to be readily available 24 hours a day for guests staying in suites.

Breakfast was brought on a trolley to my room, and as I drew back the drapes a cheerful sunbeam fell across the bed and the great trees outside were coming into delicate springtime leaf. I found a toaster had been thoughtfully provided for me, so that my toast would be fresh and piping hot when I needed it.

Clearly, the Milestone truly understands that details like this are exactly what makes a hotel visit memorable and will encourage a visitor to return.

Memorable, too, are the special 'themed' suites, like the Safari, with its incredible tented ceiling and colonial fan, or the quintessentially English Tudor Suite, which has a four-poster bed, leaded windows and a minstrel's gallery. In the Club Suite, a full-size antique billiards table awaits you!

In the evening, the Milestone's exclusive restaurant, Cheneston's, offers traditional cuisine and a wide selection of fine wines that match your opulent surroundings. You can, as I did, dine from the same menu in the less formal Park Lounge and ask for your after-dinner coffee and liqueurs to be brought to you in the romantic conservatory. The Milestone is an aristocratic celebration of the English experience, a stately home conveniently transported to the centre of London, and a dream to savour…

GREAT EASTERN HOTEL

rightly claim to be a modern British classic.

Conveniently adjacent to Liverpool Street Station and on the eastern edge of Britain's financial nerve-centre, the exterior of the Great Eastern recaptures its original grandeur and immensity, yet, within, its magical and stylish design is intimate and cosy.

There are 267 rooms, 21 suites, five very distinctive restaurants and 12 private dining suites, yet a wonderful feeling of individuality persists. No two guest rooms are alike. On the two brand-new upper floors, there is a light-filled 'loft' feel to the rooms, others are detailed with typically ornate late-Victorian features or are modern, restrained, almost minimal. But they all offer luxuriously comfortable surroundings and a full complement of up-to-the-minute services: workstations, two-line phones, faxes, voicemail and datapools, as well as recreational facilities such as satellite television, CD and DVD players, personal mini-bars and even in-room aromatherapy facilities.

The name of this hotel, the only one in the square mile of the City financial district, is redolent of railway travel in the first part of the 20th century, when, across the country, any town with a station would have a Railway Hotel close by…

and there are many deliberate design references in the new Great Eastern Hotel that recall and celebrate the richness of first class carriages in those early Victorian years.

The Great Eastern was built in 1884 and is itself an icon from the golden age of steam. Two years ago a major programme of reconstruction and restoration was begun and in February 2000 the Great Eastern re-opened and can

Each of the restaurants housed within the Great Eastern have a very individual identity and their own separate entrances. Aurora, the flagship restaurant, is a lovely space, defined by its dramatic stained-glass dome; back-lit after dark, it must surely be one of London's most beautiful dining rooms. Aurora promises to be rigorous in pursuit of excellence. Meat, poultry and game, prepared in classic European styles, will be signature dishes and desserts will be a speciality. Unusually, Aurora will be open for breakfast, as

well as lunch and dinner.
Terminus food is quick and simple but cosmopolitan and delicious; its atmosphere stylish, bright and informed. Try their grills, rotisseries, pastas and risottos.

Fishmarket, as you'd guess, is the place for seafood lovers and Miyabi is a Japanses venue; sushi, sashimi and tempura are increasingly popular these days with informed Londoners.

George offers a lovely Victorian room, full of quirky characterfulness, serving hearty traditional English food - steak and kidney pies, pot roasts, casseroles, smoked hams and roast beef sandwiches.

All in all, the new Great Eastern Hotel provides an exciting top-quality social and culinary epicentre not just for the City, but all of London.

SANDERSON

One of the most innovative influences on the London hotel scene comes from American Ian Schrager. St. Martins Lane came first and now we have an even more original creation to enjoy. In Berners Street, not far south of Regent's Park and within the northern boundaries of Soho, within easy walking distance of West End shops and theatres, is the incredible Sanderson Hotel.

Schrager himself, and quite without hyperbole, calls the Sanderson an 'urban spa', an lavish dreamscape, a balancing act between extravagance and simplicity. "It's an hotel," he says, "for modern people who crave something original, different… and magical!"

You'll find charm at Sanderson, glamour and elegance, a witty dollop of excess, and even poetry. But there's also some straightforward cosiness that will have you wriggling out of your shoes and heaving a sigh of contentment.

Enter by the theatrical front door, and the sense of dream and other-worldliness begins. In front of you sits, invitingly, a wonderfully curvaceous Salvador Dali red lips sofa, and a swathe of 18th century silver silk opera curtains. As you step across the lovely maple wood floor, there's a front desk that will astonish, even mesmerize you… a bank of video monitors are playing an ever-changing montage of images by video artists from across the world. And there's another surreal touch: a Louis XIV-style sofa that is 35 feet long!

No sooner have you taken in these fantastical details than you'll encounter the lush oasis of the Courtyard Garden, open to the sometimes fickle sky but a wonderful place, in good weather, to meet with friends, to eat, drink and socialize.

A huge 40-foot magnolia
spreads protective arms over
chuckling fountains, a serene
reflective pool and scores of
trees and flowering perennials
set in huge terracotta pots and
galvanised steel planters.
All these elegantly-realised, rad-
ical designs continue throughout the hotel. The guest rooms
are equally stirring and beautiful, soft and sensuous.

individual room (there are 150 in all) is unencumbered by interior walls, so the sense of space is unparallelled. The bathroom and dressing room are separated only by glass and luxurious silk curtains, which can be controlled electronically by the guest.

There are wonderful facilities at your disposal at the Sanderson. The magical Aqua Bathhouse for example, tranquil and white, light, ethereal and nurturing. Ancient eastern traditions are seamlessly blended with cutting-edge technological developments. You'll leave feeling rested and rejuventated.

The gourmet restaurant Spoon+ offers a limitless mix and match menu, orchestrated by head chef Alain Duchesse. You can choose to be served in the Courtyard Garden, at the 80-foot long onyx bar, in the exquisite dining room itself, or in the restful privacy of your own room. Wherever you choose, you will be entranced. The wonderful interior of the Sanderson was designed in collaboration with Philippe Starck, and the result is intimate, restful, and full of wit - pure magic!

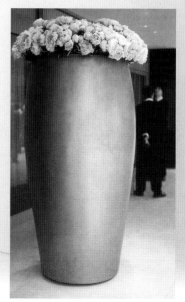

THE NEW VEERASWAMY RESTAURANT

These days, a party of Englishmen eating out are much more likely to step into an Indian restaurant than seek out traditional fare such as roast beef and Yorkshire pudding. But they will not, as a rule, be eating a meal an Indian on the sub-continent would recognise.

In Regent Street, however, a restaurant can be found that offers the true Indian culinary experience, and it will be a mouth-watering delight. The New Veeraswamy is a wonderfully stylish reincarnation of almost certainly the oldest Indian restaurant in Britain. It was established 72 years ago and was long hailed as a fashionable and conveniently central Indian eating-house, host to many well-known figures, including Pandit Nehru and Indira Ghandi.

How do they achieve their authenticity? By inviting experienced chefs to join the team direct from India, by importing the highest quality regional spices and grinding them freshly for each and every dish. The atmosphere at the Veeraswamy is a far cry from the rather dim-lit and hackneyed environment one might normally encounter in an Indian restaurant these days. It is very contemporary, fresh and airy, colourful and clean - and the service is attentive and friendly.

I found making any choice difficult, but eventually settled for a Dum ka Murgh, a mellow chicken curry dish with yoghurt, poppy seeds, mint, nuts and saffron. There were plenty of side dishes on offer, too, together with a delicious a la carte dessert menu and an excellent wine list.

The Veeraswamy, being so conveniently central, would be a wonderful choice for anyone planning an evening at the theatre, and you should consider taking advantage of several theatre/dining packages available. Ticketselect (on 0207.494.5494) always have a selection and the Peter Hall Company at the Piccadilly Theatre (0207.369.1734) offer similarly interesting discounts. You could find yourself dining at the stylish Veeraswamy for virtually nothing at all.

There is only one disadvantage: after the experience of a visit to this high-quality eating-house, you may find eating at any other Indian restaurant you try out rather less than perfect…

QUO VADIS

The name of this restaurant reminds me more of the brutal clash of swords than the delicate click of silver cutlery, but a name is barely material when a place can so easily make a name for itself as Quo Vadis has done.

Two high-profile figures are associated with Quo Vadis in its first incarnation: volatile chef Marco Pierre White and artist Damien Hirst, he of the infamous pickled sheep. It took a brave diner to set aside their fiercesome reputations, but there must have been many, for Quo Vadis, even lacking a question mark, soon became one of the chic-to-be-seen-at places for the person-about-town. Even its somewhat seedy location, in Dean Street, Soho, couldn't deter the determinedly fashionable.

The cuisine is certainly one of the reasons for securing yourself a booking here. Once you've made your Hogarthian way to its door, been charmed by your welcome relieved to f!nd you've managed to procure a 'good' table, struck up a rapport with your server and chosen a satisfactory aperitif to open proceedings, then an encounter with the menu is the next pleasure in line.

The menu these days is reasonably simple; short enough to find your way through, yet with sufficient choices, and interesting enough ones, to give a diner pleasurable pause.

I plumped for risotto calamari that was full of flavours and, to my mind, perfectly cooked, in the true Italian mode. My wife, a great fan of lobster, found the Quo Vadis version plump and succulent, as good, she told me, as any anywhere… no, she thoughtfully amended… better. Prices, at least if you are sparing with your wines, offer excellent value and after you've lingered over your coffee watching the drama of Quo Vadis quietly unfold, I'd suggest - even if it means a detour - a mellow stroll across to Soho's Chinatown, to spice your evening out with a last colourful dénouement before the curtain falls.

To my mind, a make-over of the decor, a re-think over pricing and a new, revitalised menu, even a new tribe of regulars, have wrought wonderful imporvements. Fernando Piere has been tempted from the Ivy to front the restyled Quo Vadis and, in consequence, the atmosphere now is relaxed and friendly.

THE GASTRODROME

In the swashbuckling era of the clipper ships, Butler's Wharf, on the once less favoured south side of the River Thames, was where the merchant adventurers tied up and unloaded their crates of pungent spices and teas from the mysterious East, barrels of French wine and cocoa beans from Africa. The lanes and alleys that surrounded the wharves were noisy and Dickensian, crammed with the riff-raff of London's East End, full of eager and dangerous life. After World War II, shipping went elsewhere, most notably to Rotterdam and Antwerp, and there followed a slow and melancholy decline, until finally the whole area was abandoned to rust and to the rats. It took someone with the vision, energy and daring of Terence Conran to see the possibilities of the site. But even he found it difficult at first to interest other businessmen in his ideas.

Today, at last, these forgotten acres, in the shadow of Tower Bridge, have been restored and are a popular destination to rival Covent Garden. The whole run-down Docklands area has discovered a new lease of life. The development has been concluded with a range of top-drawer apartments.

The Gastrodrome is not just one restaurant, but a clutch of them, each with its own special atmosphere and its own keynote specialities.

The Blue Print Café was the first of them, paving the way for its elegant sisters Le Pont de la Tour, Cantina del Ponte and the Butler's Wharf Chop House…

But this is not all: the celebration of good food is taken yet further. There are five shops, too, at the Gastrodrome, selling everyday staples, seafood and adventurous wines. In fine weather, the Gastrodrome seats 750 customers. Tables spill out onto the riverfront terraces. The shops and restaurants, different in spirit as they may be, share a common modernist aesthetic. The kitchens are open to view, some industrial finishes are left intact and form intertwines cleverly with function.

The Design Musuem has been moved to the site from the Victoria and Albert Museum in South Kensington and the Blue Print Café can be found on the first floor, at the heart of the museum. There's a relaxed atmosphere and the food is excellent. Chef Jeremy Lee has a passion for the very freshest of ingredients, simply prepared.

His influences are eclectic, ranging across the world, from California to the Mediterranean and the Middle East.

Butler's Wharf Chop House is reminiscent of a cricket pavillion or rather, given its riverside location, a boat-house, with a mixture of oak, elm and ash for the flooring, tables and chairs, which creates a warm and uncluttered atmosphere.

Game in season, succulent Welsh lamb and the very best Aberdeen Angus beef are amongst chef David Hollins' specialities, together with fish and crustaceans from British rivers and the seas around the coast.

Cantina del Ponte, as you might expect from its name, is a Mediterranean-influenced restaurant. Quality pizzas, prepared in a wood-fired oven, complement a selection of excellent pastas and other Italian dishes.

Finally, to round off the cluster of restaurants on the Gastrodrome site, there's the highly-thought-of Le Pont de la Tour, named after the richly decorative 19th century Tower Bridge that rises majestically skyward just outside the windows. It is an outstanding restaurant with a very British menu that has influences of French and Italian regional cooking. The present Prime Minister Tony Blair once entertained Bill Clinton here.

There's always a wide selection of fish, lobsters, langoustines and oysters on the menu. Le Pont de la Tour encapsulates the spirit of the Gastrodrome itself, offering a bar and grill, and the opportunity to shop at the specialist bakery and the wine merchants, which has no less than 600 different wines available in an atmospheric vault-like space with a graceful, arched ceiling.

The Gastrodrome is a conveniently short walk across the river from the teeming financial quarter we know simply as the City, and at lunchtime city types take full advantage of the new and welcome food destination on their doorstep.

The Gastrodrome is too exciting and too individual to be missed. The daring optimism of a decade ago has been triumphantly confirmed. The romantic swashbuckling days of the East India Company have returned, rousingly, to the banks of old Father Thames.

LIVEBAIT

If anybody needs proof that these days, the world is a global village, Livebait chef Martin Manning is a perfect example. From his Notting Hill restaurant, Martin can e-mail a supplier in Australia, who will relay a message to fishermen working off the coast. Within minutes, a message may reach him saying that a very special fish has been caught - a 'cricket ball' tuna perhaps, with eyes big enough to fit neatly into the palm of an Australian fast bowler - and that very fish will be on Martin's menu 36 hours later. "My customers," says Martin, "love exotic fish and new adventurous dishes!" Livebait now has five restaurants in London and they all offer innovative recipes and unusual fish and seafood in addition to all the longstanding and popular varieties. You'll find a branch in Covent Garden as well as in Notting Hill; and one not far from there in Westbourne Grove; another outside Waterloo station; the most recent one near St. Paul's Cathedral, in the City, and Livebait's Café Fish, just off Shaftesbury Avenue, which cuts through Soho. Each one of them is building up an enthusiastic clientele of regulars, both for business lunch-times and the evening crowd, who would be well-advised to contact Livebait before making a theatre booking, because Livebait do some attractive theatre/restaurant deals. A nice balance has been struck at Livebait between the needs of a popular restaurant, happy to offer a cheaper two- or three-course set menu and one especially for children, as well as satisfying the requirements of an establishment offering fine gourmet food, and the prices clearly represent excellent value for money.

My favourite dish, currently, is monkfish, and it was simply and deliciously prepared at Livebait Covent Garden, served with a tarragon cream sauce, wild mushrooms and a tasty Thaï risotto, with a side-dish of mangetout peas with black bean and ginger.

At Livebait Notting Hill my wife joined me in their extensive Livebait Platter, a seafood collection that included whole Dorset brown crab, Nova Scotia lobster, white crevettes from Saudi Arabia, langoustines and juicy Atlantic prawns, served with sautéd new potatoes and a roquette and parmesan salad.

There are some cheerfully characterful British beers on offer, and they were evidently very popular, but there are also some excellent wines to choose from.

Livebait have received a clutch of prestigious culinary awards in their short life, including the London magazine Time Out's Best Newcomer of the Year in 1996 and Best Service of the Year in 1997.

I kept wondering what it was that seems so familiar in these prestigious surroundings. The white tiles jolted my memory: there is a down-to-earth *joie de vivre* that links Livebait to its Cockney ancestor, the Pie and Eel shop!

By the way: if you've enjoyed the Livebait experience, then their Livebait Cookbook would be an endlessly satisfying souvenir to carry away with you.

QUAGLINO'S

Quaglino's was a dazzling restaurant all the way back in the 'thirties, a living theatre where the darlings of society played out their glamorous games to the twinkle of chandeliers and the tinkle of wine glasses. After a £3 million refurbishment, it was re-opened on Valentine's Day, 1993, a glittering new star of the Terence Conran group, and it's again the swanky destination of London's youthful coterie of successful men and women making a name for themselves in a wide spectrum of endeavours, from business to the arts. This is the place to come to when you've arrived... or are likely to, very soon!

The food and service reflect the achievements of London itself. A centre for so much else, it has now become a gastronomic centre, too. The menu at Quaglino's is contemporary and European, its inspiration the brasseries and café society of old Paris - bohemian, intellectual and aristocratic all at once, they welcomed anyone, no questions asked.

The entertainment at Quaglino's, just as it was in Paris, is not to be found only in the cuisine or in the wine cellar, which is carefully stocked but not extensive. Equally important are the ambience and the particular design features. Quaglino's has an unimpressive entranceway, but it opens out into a spectacular subterranean cavern, swirling vividly with life and colour and wafting with exciting aromas from the open kitchens. You reach it by a sweeping central staircase just made for the grand entrance. The main restaurant can seat 300 or so, and the bar 90, yet because of the generous scale of the place, you don't feel uncomfortable. For those who would prefer privacy on a particular occasion, there is a lovely private dining room.

For a place so large, the brasserie food is excellent and served quickly. My spinach and Parmesan tart was delicious, my companion's lobster salad equally impressive. We finished with an outstanding crème brûlée before sitting back with a cup of arabica coffeee and happily watching the ebb and flow of the in-crowd.

MOMO'S

Momo is the nickname given by his friends to Mourad Mazouz, Algerian-born of Berber parents, whose whirlwind rise to fame in the world of gastronomy has been one of the events of the past few years. He opened his first restaurant, Bascow, in Paris, and followed his runaway initial success with 404, named tongue-in-cheek after the workman-like Peugeot model used all over North Africa as a taxi. He considered it time, then, to look across the Channel and tackle the London scene… and so Momo's was born, in a typical blaze of publicity, with a party thrown by Madonna and attended by the likes of Naomi Campbell and Stella McCartney. Since then, Momo's has been one of those places the fashionable must be seen at.

The food at Momo's is North African, with couscous, succulent lamb and fresh Mediterranean vegetables a popular choice. But youthful Moroccan-born chef Michel Giraud has effortlessly lifted the cuisine far beyond run-of-the-mill preconceptions. His pastilla, tagines and couscous-based dishes are infused with something very special, an insider's knowledge of secrets gleaned from the traditions of his own family.

Good food, of course, is a prerequisite for any successful restaurant… but these days customers are looking for that something extra in terms of ambience; they want more than just a meal out. So Momo hired a DJ, Francis Peyrat. Francis and Momo made music an integral part of the whole Momo's experience and have introduced diners to their own special mix of world music that

has come to be called 'arabesque'.

His staff, too, are singularly different. They have somewhat elevated the plain task of providing good, friendly, swift service to one of the arts, with a cool and funky style that echoes the music coming over the speakers. Those who don't wish to actually eat at Momo's make their way downstairs to the Kemia Bar, where younger people from all walks of life, of every colour and creed, mix

together to create a special atmosphere that is vivid and exciting.

Next door to Momo's is his newest project, called simply Mö - a typically Moroccan tea-shop, serving traditional mint tea, a selection of less familiar teas, and sweet Maghrebi pastries. Disposed around the tea-shop you'll find for sale some of the North African artifacts and ethnic furniture Momo has gathered on travels back to his homeland. Soon to join them will be Momo's lifestyle and cookery book… then you'll be able to take home with you a little bit of the Momo magic.

YO! SUSHI

What I like most about the new spirit in the restaurant and hotel business in great cities like London and New York, Paris and Los Angeles, is that it possesses a youthful and contagious lightheartedness and vivacious chumminess, a lack of pretension, whilst in the best entrepreneurial tradition nevertheless providing a quality product and top-class customer service.

This gift for joyful optimism and fresh vision is encapsulated in Yo! Sushi and its downstairs bar Yo! Below.

Situated in Poland Street, in London's lively and colourful

Soho district, Yo! Sushi is the Japanese experience given an imaginative and sparkling spin. Your visit here will not be only an adventure into the raw, cool… and healthy world of sushi, but into the very heart of

cool London fashion too. The ambience at Yo! Sushi has been dubbed 'performance art' and 'futuristic dining' - but don't let this relentlessly trendy image put you off: you will be fed very well, there's no question of that, and with great panache. Sushi may be one of the most trendy foods of today, but the secret of good sushi lies in traditional values: the use of the best, freshest ingredients, combined with the uttermost care. And what is served here, is nothing but the best. At Yo! Sushi there are many varieties

121

of sushi to choose from, but each of them is a tiny work of art, a combination of the most delicate of flavours.

And when you've finished your meal, don't leave. Take yourself downstairs to Yo! Below, their new high-tech cellar bar, and soak in the atmosphere. You might not find yourself a place to sit, but it will be a memorable experience all the same. You may even encounter one of your favourite show-business personalities at the bar, for the guest list reads like a celebrity Who's Who. Michael Douglas dropped in, and Naomi Campbell, Kate Moss, Pete Townsend, Madonna, Stella McCartney and many more. Simon Woodroffe, driving force behind the enterprise, has won a clutch of awards for his design and his revolutionary concepts, including Emerging Entrepreneur of the year 1999, and the Design Week Prize in 1998 for Restaurants, Bars and Clubs.

He has clearly not reached a culmination of his ambitions yet, for he says: "The Yo! identity was always unlikely to be the simple identity of a sushi bar - but a whole brand concept." We're clearly only at the beginning of the Yo! story… with a whole millennium ahead of us!

OXO TOWER RESTAURANT, BAR & BRASSERIE

Harvey Nichols opened its famous Knightsbridge store in 1813. Its restaurant business has now expanded beyond that original site to a spectacular location on London's South Bank, where many new and exciting architectural projects can be found, such as the new Tate gallery and the dramatic, slowly spinning London Eye. The South Bank is always alive with colour and music, and every season offers a different view of London life at its best. The design of Oxo Tower, by architects Lifschutz Davidson, takes elegantly into account the original Art Deco building in which it is housed, as well as the silver-flowing waters of the River Thames below. You feel as if you might be on some 1930s ocean-going liner.

The restaurant's huge windows are cleverly designed to prevent night-time reflections interfering with diners' enjoyment of the outstanding riverside views.

Head chef Simon Arkless has moved to Oxo Tower from Fifth Floor, its sister restaurant in Knightsbridge. His cuisine is a wonderful mix of traditional and comtemporary and Oxo Tower offers him an appropriate high profile showcase for his enormous talents.

The wine list, presided over by head sommelier Robert Giorgione, is remarkable and very extensive… ask him for his advice and he may come up with something as spectacular as the view laid out before you.

The Bar, with its blue leather upholstery and high chromed stools, serves classic and contemporary cocktails, together with the entire sparkling range of wines available to patrons of the restaurant, and there are equally wonderful views from the south side of Oxo Tower. The Brasserie is a modern, exciting and colourful space, with bright furnishings, lots of stainless steel and polished wood. Australian Cait Mitchelhill is head chef here and her dishes reflect her multicultural influences and magic Mediterranean touch. Whether you choose an extensive, leisurely dinner in the Restaurant, or a fashionable, equally tasty meal in the Brasserie, you are guaranteed a wonderful culinary experience, brought to you by friendly, professional staff. And with such views to accompany each bite, there is an unparalelled sense of occasion to any visit to Oxo Tower. Here, you will truly feel on top of the world.

RULES

In an energetic and vital city like London which enthusiastically remakes its image in concert with the times, there are few restaurants that have reached, indeed surpassed, their bicentennary.

One such is Rules, in Covent Garden. You could not guess, from its name alone, at the romance of its starstudded past. In 1798, the year Napoleon set out upon his Egyptian campaign, one Thomas Rule put aside the indiscretions of his wayward youth… and opened an oyster bar.

To the happy surprise of his long-suffering parents, Thomas' enterprise thrived and became an eating-and-meeting-place of consequence, attracting to its door - as one contemporary writer put it - "the rakes, dandies and superior intelligences" of the day.

Rules flourishes still, surviving even the wholesale redevelopment of the Covent Garden area - in great part due to the fervent support of the celebrated poet and antiquarian John Betjeman.

One of several dining rooms at Rules bears his name, in gratitude. Another takes the name of Graham Greene, who year after year enjoyed celebrating his birthday at Rules… and mentioned the restaurant in several of his books.

Throughout its long history, the tables at Rules have been crowded with writers, artists, journalists and actors. Charles Dickens, Thackeray, John Galsworthy, Evelyn Waugh, the great actor Henry Irving and, in more recent times, thriller writer John Le Carré, Laurence Olivier, Clark Gable, Charlie Chaplin and Buster Keaton all enjoyed the food and the

atmosphere here. The past lives on at Rules, recorded on the walls in hundreds of drawings, paintings and cartoons.

Rules has been gloriously unwavering in its celebration of traditional English food. 'Porter, pies and oysters' were staples at Rules at the end of the 18th century and today you will still

find pies and puddings on the menu, oysters too, of course, and all the classic game - rabbit, pheasant, venison, grouse and duck. Much of the game comes from an estate in the Pennines in Yorkshire which is owned by Rules itself. You can even put together a party of six and go game-shooting there. Lartington Hall Park, near Barnard Castle in Teesdale, is an ideal venue for the adventurous, and there is a comfortable shooting lodge on the estate available for hire during the spring and summer.

Rules would be the ideal place to take a friend from faraway who is sceptical about British food - it would be amusing to watch him eat his words here! Though a committed vegetarian would have a difficult time at this wonderful restaurant, redolent with history and alive with passion for great food prepared in the time-honoured manner, the rest of us can be assured of an unforgettable evening.

FIFTH FLOOR RESTAURANT

Harvey Nichols is shopping heaven. The designer fashion store offers clothes by great names from all over the world, from Japan to America and the best of Europe. It is set in fashionable Knightsbridge, not far from Harrods, another must-visit for shoppers with taste and the right budget. In 1992, the store was purchased by Dickson Poon, of Dickson Concepts, based in Hong Kong. It has been his vision to take Harvey Nichols into two new and hopefully very profitable areas: a state-of-the-art food market, to rival Harrods' own, and an important restaurant, bar and café group. After all, ladies who shop are also ladies who lunch, dine and cook. The style of the in-store restaurant and food market on the fifth floor was seen as complementary to its high fashion image. The Fifth Floor Restaurant is indeed a triumph and already a market leader. For gourmets in the know, this restaurant might even be the reason for their visit and the clothes shopping an incidental…

The design of the Fifth Floor restaurant is subtle and elegant, with lovely floors fashioned from reclaimed teak parquet. There are fine views over the bustling streets of Knightsbridge below, and if you want to, you can take a lift straight up and miss out on the clothes completely - although that would be a pity.

Head chef in the restaurant is Henry Harris, a creative cook in the best sense of the word. He has been involved with Fifth Floor since it opened, and even before: he was in the enviable position of being able to assist in planning the layout of his kitchen. It's not easy to sum up a chef's cooking style in a word or two - but traditional French bistro would possibly be accurate, with a discreet and discernable Mediterranean influence.

If your meal at the Fifth Floor restaurant was as memorable as ours, you may wish to carry off a copy of the chef's own Fifth Floor cookbook, and try out some of his wonderful recipes at home. You can

always shop for the right ingredients in Harvey Nichols' own gourmet food market, found conveniently under the same roof.

VONG

The Berkeley Hotel, in Knightsbridge, is the venue for one of the most exciting experiences in cuisine presently available in London.

Vong, named after its celebrated chef-proprietor Jean-Georges Vongerichten, a native of Alsace, is something unexpected - a Thai restaurant with French undertones. Jean-Georges has often been called a genius by food enthusiasts, and a visit to Vong, a very short stroll from Hyde Park Corner, will - if he is in the kitchen - explain just why. If Thai food has let you down somewhat in the past, forget the word and let's call Vong a 'Pacific Rim' experience. There's no fat, no butter or cream, no heavy use of the pepper shaker, or even of lemongrass, just a clever,

even witty, mingling of traditional Western meats and seafood, such as veal and lobster, with cunningly-mixed aromatic Eastern spices and herbs. Signature dishes are a surprisingly delicate chicken and coconut soup, sautéed *foie gras* with ginger and mango and a wonderful rabbit curry from which every bone has been carefully removed. I chose the latter, and ended a beautiful meal with a wonderful array of *crème brûlées*, each of them differently flavoured, each of them delicious in its own way.

Vong is more, much more than just a place to go for a meal out. It is an adventure for the tastebuds… and you should make adventurous choices. You will not be disappointed!

Wines? Well, there's an international selection, as you'd expect, but with an especially wide choice of Alsace wines from Jean-Georges' homeland, which go particularly well with his cuisine.

Vong has been designed with great flair and impact by Keith Hobbs and Linzi Coppick, of United Designers, who created Conran's Gastrodrome restaurant Le Pont de la Tour, Quaglino's and Mezzo. Colours of fabrics and even the staff's snazzy waiscoats echo the colours of the oriental spices arranged on the waiters' stat-

ion. You can view the theatre of the kitchen through a plate-glass window as you await your meal.

"The flavours of cilantro, lemongrass, ginger, curries, and coconut milk changed my life," Jean-Georges Vongerichten has been quoted as saying. Now it's the turn of his fortunate customers to delight in the culinary wizardry born of his love affair with the East.

BELGO ZUID

It was not so long ago that Londoners would have to have travelled across the Channel to sample the Belgian culinary experience… but Belgium, with its full-bodied, potent and tasty beers and its piled plates of steaming fresh-cooked mussels, has come to them.

Belgo Zuid is the third London restaurant with a very Belgian touch, opened after the tremendous succes of Belgo Noord, in Chalk Farm Road near Camden Town, and Belgo Centraal, in the Covent Garden area. And yes, we are told, it was a risk to introduce mussels to the English, for they are an acquired taste. But Belgo became an instant hit, especially with the fashionable young, who did not just taste the mus-

sels there, but also enjoyed the vast selection of Belgian speciality beers.

Belgo Zuid, in Ladbroke Grove, is the most recent to open in the capital. Each Belgo restaurant has its own very individual design, and differing menus, but the food is absolutely and uniformly Belgian. Mussels, of course, are the signature dish and are served in 10 different ways, but there's plenty more seafood - such as no less than six delicious crab dishes - and many varieties of rich sausages - try wild boar! - and authentic dishes such as *carbonnades flamandes*, beef braised in beer, with apples and prunes.

The Belgians lay just claim to the invention of the ubiquitous chip, but their version, slim and dry, puts the usual English offering to shame. Eat them with mayonaise, naturally! Yes, the food is stunning, traditional and inventive all at once, and the beers are available in a hundred varieties, all packing a punch, with plenty of flavour. The new Ladbroke Grove Belgo is built within the framework of an incredible but dilapidated dance hall, that provided a great space for a stylish and spectacularly inventive design that pays homage to two great Belgian sporting icons - cyclist Eddy Merckx and racing driver Jacky Ickx. The bar, located directly aboven the open plan fiery-red kitchen, was inspired by 16th century painter

Hieronymus Bosch' images of heaven and hell… But don't let that frighten you off, for the effect is stunning. Some will go to Belgo Zuid for the atmosphere alone - but they will find heaven on their plates here, and return time and again.

FISH!

The name's a simple one, succinct and to the point and the menu offered by this bright new brasserie is simple, too - the freshest fish, cooked straightforwardly and swiftly. One clever innovation is that the customer can choose how his fish is cooked, steamed or grilled, and with what sauce. There's organic salmon on the menu, snapper, sea bass and squid, monkfish and mullet, turbot and tuna. You may feel like trying a spaghetti tuna bolognese, fish sausages, perhaps, with mashed potato, a grilled lobster and chips or a swordfish club sandwich.

There are already two locations in London to choose from, both cleverly placed. The first is in the City, at bustling Borough Market, in the shadow of elegant Southwark Cathedral, and the second, only recently opened, is in Battersea, now an up-and-coming area, its little streets of terraced houses now awash with media professionals and expensive dot.com types.

Fish! at Borough Market is situated on a lively corner site within a Victorian pavilion building that's been transformed by architect Julyan Wickham into a contemporary, light-filled and airy space, using a palette of associative aquatic blues.

There are 90 interior seats and a further 60, for those sunnier days, out on the terrace that looks across to Southwark Cathedral.

The team responsible for the whole concept has been brought together by owners Tony Allan and Ronnie Truss, who opened the succesful Bank restaurant in 1996. They include William Black, consultant and co-author, with his wife television chef Sophie Grigson, of the popular Fish cookbook, Michelin-starred director of food Christian Deiteil and front of house director Eric Garnier. There's a hefty measure of ecological sensitivity in the Fish! venture. William Black has long had a particular interest in sustainable sources of healthy fish and the proper conservation of this 'last great wild food source'.

He says: "With so many of the world's fisheries under pressure from habitat destruction, overfishing and poor management, we are seeking ways to encourage responsible practice. At fish! we work alongside the Marine Stewardship Council (MSC) and the World Wildlife Fund's Endangered Seas Campaign, and we try whenever possible to use MSC-certified sources."

Tony Allan was himself a chef and became dissatisfied with the quality of fish then at his disposal. He set up his own fish supply service, driving to the Channel ports to buy for himself, straight from the trawlers, the best fish he could find. Not surprisingly, fish! has become a hugely successful endeavour. Next door, you'll find a retail outlet offering the same high quality fish you'll find on your plate in the diner. Busy people, thinking ahead to their supper, can make credit card orders over the phone and pick up their purchases, already wrapped, on their way home from work. A wonderful initiative, and one more reason why the exclamation mark behind fish! is richly deserved.

JULIE'S RESTAURANT

Anyone staying at the Portobello Hotel will eventually need to eat something and will be required to drag himself away from his state-of-the-art guest room. But there'll be no need for him to travel any distance.

Just around the corner, in nearby Portland Road is Julie's, a restaurant with the same distinctive design flair as the Portobello. Which should really be no surprise, because its proprietors are Tim and Cathy Herring, who also own the Portobello hotel… and guests of the hotel will be favoured with a very useful 10% reduction on their bill when they eat at Julie's.

Julie's opened over thirty years ago, in 1969, and was designed by Julie Hodgess, who also created the decor for Biba's, the clothing store once at the very cutting edge of British fashion. There are five very different themed rooms to choose from - six, if you count the pavement side terrace. The regal, dark-shadowed medieval Banqueting Room will make you feel like an honoured guest in an ancient castle, with its huge oval dining table, ranks of softly glowing candles, antique tapestries and, surprisingly, a pulpit - from which, I'm assured, speeches are still delivered.

In summer, on long, light evenings, the airy Garden Room might be a good choice - an elegant wrought-iron staircase winding upwards, populations of lush green plants and the doors thrown open onto a cool and secret little garden. There's the Gothic Room, too, with tall-backed chairs to sit on and heavy muffling drapes, the fern-hung Julie's Bar, and finally the enigmatically-named Back Room… who knows what personage might be secluded there, with his companions? And the food itself is the best reason for being here.

Executive chef Johnny Ekperigin presides over a cuisine best described as 'modern English'. Gone are the heavy creamy sauces of yesterday, replaced by ones that are light and natural, full of flavour but happily low in cholesterol.

During my visit, the new 'summer menu' was on offer, to be replaced in late autumn by an equally exciting 'winter menu'. I started off with a feather-light crab and cucumber mousse with purée of green olives, beautifully presented, with that perfect Mediterranean touch that suits a British summer evening just as well. For my main dish, I decided on grilled balsamic chicken with pumpkin sauce and fried ginger. Julie's crème brûlée and some good strong coffee concluded a meal that was tasty and plentiful and yet did not lie heavily on the stomach. Combined with a friendly staff, a good wine list and a wonderful ambience they make Julie's a restaurant to revisit, whether you stay at the Portobello or not.

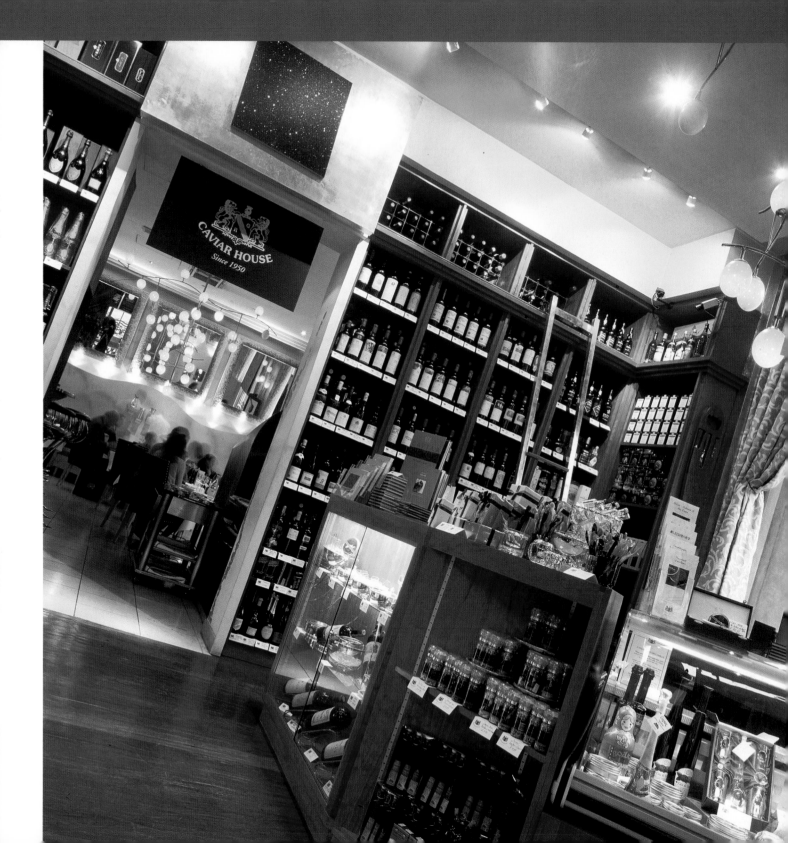

CAVIAR HOUSE

They are poetically known as 'the jewels of the sea'. Tiny, black, glowing eggs that bewitch the afficionado; rare, exotic… and expensive.

Exactly half a century ago, in 1950, Georges Rebeiz, the founder of Caviar House, received two small tins of caviar as a gift from distant Persia. He noticed with surprise how this delicacy from afar delighted and excited his friends and, impulsively or astutely, we'll never know which, he opened in Copenhagen his first outlet for this wonderful food from the belly of the Belgua sturgeon – itself a rare enough freshwater fish, found only in the inland waters of the giant Caspian Sea.

Caviar House has expanded vigorously since then… and in unusual settings, such as airports. Its range of products, too, has developed far beyond caviar alone, but the spirit of luxury, good taste and excellent quality had informed the business at every stage. From city centre 'boutiques' to airport shops and then seafood bars, Caviar House now offers the discerning gourmet quality restaurants also, in which he can consume their particular delicacies in appropriately sophisticated surroundings. In St. James's Street, Piccadilly, you'll find the English flagship store and restaurant, the perfect encapsulation of the Caviar House ethos.

As soon as you step through the door of Caviar House, you enter a world of calm and privilege. Quality teas and fine coffees, liqueurs, special cheeses, top-grade olive oils, the best biscuits and confectionary, homemade *foie gras*, black French truffles, champagne, the great whiskies, cognacs and even the finest Belgian chocolates, each of them will be delightfully packaged as rare gifts in presentation boxes. There is Balik salmon, the choicest of fillets washed in clear spring water and smoked by a particular method in the mountains of Switzerland - it comes highly recommended.

And then there is, of course, the caviar.

If you have time to spare, then find a table in the Caviar House restaurant and treat yourself to a little luxury. You may find a new passion: for the dark jewels of the sea, or for a particular roast of a particular coffee bean perhaps. You may well make a decision never again to be content with second best. Not after having tasted what Caviar House has to offer.

WOKWOK

In a lively and vivid cosmopolitan melting-pot like London, you can take a trip around the world without shelling out for anything more than a few taxi fares. The spirit of far-flung countries is often summed up in their food and across the capital you can discover a wealth of restaurants that offer plenty of opportunity to travel, albeit by taste-bud alone, to every corner of the globe. One such is wok.wok, an exciting adventure into the Asian culinary experience, so successful that from its first incarnation in the Fulham Road, there are now five restaurants across London… and three more out in the regions.

The inspiration behind wok.wok comes from the exotic depths of Asia - from the steamy and jostling market lanes of Hong Kong, the aromatic spice markets of Thailand, the terraced rice paddies of Indonesia and the romantic lantern-lit night markets of Kuala Lumpur and Singapore.

Creator of wok.wok is Tania Webb, who brings a wealth of first-hand experience and lots of new exciting ideas from her sojourns in Malaysia and Hong Kong. "The fantastic thing about Asian cuisines," she says, "is that you can mix and match - Vietnamese rice paper rolls, say, with Chinese dumplings and Singapore *laksa*, and satisfy all your cravings in one meal!" Part of the immediate delight is in the superb modern minimalist designs you'll find at any wok.wok, the work of architects Derek Wylie. Gleaming metal, fresh and light oak flooring and bold colours combine with the captivating aromas of the open kitchen where a band of chefs put on a show full of theatrical grace as, in mists of steam and dangerous-looking flashes of flame they swiftly prepare each dish to order. "So good they named it twice," enthuses one reviewer. So good, also, that a single visit will lead surely to a second - and then many more.

PRISM RESTAURANT & BAR

In the last few years, high fashion store Harvey Nichols have developed a small but choice portfolio of restaurants, which include Fifth Floor in Knightsbridge and Oxo Tower on London's South Bank. Prism is their most recent development, housed in the strikingly elegant building that was formerly the Bank of New York, in the City, one of the worlds greatest and most renowned financial districts. Architects Lifschutz Davidson, who designed the hugely successful Oxo Tower restaurant, have restored this 1920s edifice back to its former glory, with classical columns, high decorated ceilings and towering windows, recreating a stunning feeling of light and space, dignity and refinement.

The restaurant and bar, together with a wonderfully romantic conservatory dining area and a suite of private dining rooms, are set on three levels in the huge 10,000 square foot space of the former banking hall.

Dominic Ford, the driving force behind the Harvey Nichols restaurant and food retail business, wisely says that "the location of our restaurants is of paramount importance" - they must offer stylish surroundings in stunning locations - and Prism is a truly dramatic and elegant space.

The furniture and fittings, too, have been chosen with great care to create a chic and luxurious atmosphere, with 1930s Mies van der Rohe 'Brno' chairs in scarlet leather and exclusively designed serving trolleys and wine coolers.

The Prism bar offers similar luxury with an elegantly contemporary accent and can be found on the lower ground floor, where the bank vaults once were. I started with an aperitif there, perched on a 'Single' bar stool designed by Frenchman Christophe Pillet, and watched trendy Londoners at play in the most elegant of environments. Then I went upstairs, to enjoy my meal.

Simon Shaw, once head chef of Harvey Nichols' Fourth Floor restaurant in Leeds, has been chosen to lead the Prism kitchen. His style has an intriguing Northern tinge - try his tempura of Whitby cod with pea purée as a starter, and there's black pudding, too, on the menu, and Cumberland sausages with brown sauce and onions; otherwise his cooking is very contemporary and international. I loved the Moroccan chicken dish, served with a fragrant lemon and parsley couscous, and Simon's pastries are particularly 'moreish'… his bitter chocolate tart with coconut sorbet was a delight.

Financiers are fortunate indeed to find a place like Prism on their doorstep - others will happily make the short trip to Leadenhall Street to enjoy the delights of this wonderful restaurant.

BLUEBIRD AT THE GASTRODROME

The Bluebird, on the King's Road, Chelsea, is an inspired extension of Terence Conran's brilliantly conceived Gastrodrome on the banks of the River Thames beneath Tower Bridge. It is, like the Gastrodrome itself, a 'food destination'. Within its walls you'll discover a foodstore, a restaurant and bar, a café, a private members' luncheon club, a Conran homeware shop, a flower stall… and an outside catering business.

Each element, as one would expect of Conran, is designed with taste and purveys, in each department, the very best available. Bluebird's meat, poultry and fine cheeses are sourced from small, usually organic, farms in the English heartland; the fish and seafood come direct from British waters.

The spectacular food store is, in fact, a community of little businesses, each run by an expert in his field, passionate about what he sells. Local Chelsea shoppers come in for ingredients for their evening meal, or they can simply sit at home, fax their orders… and wait for a Bluebird van to deliver to their door. It's a neighbourhood shop - but on the grand scale, a world away from the sterile environment of today's supermarkets.

The Bluebird is an exceptional space, tall, light and airy, with a glass roof and robust, functional girders that lend clues to the building's history… as a garage. And yes, the Bluebird in question is indeed the famous record-breaking landspeed automobile, driven by Malcolm Campbell.

The garage was built in 1923. Its original features included an art deco-like exterior with columns and enormous 'copper-lite' windows running from floor to ceiling… and these have been retained and lovingly restored. The garage forecourt now boasts an elegant steel and glass canopy where the pumps used to be. In the summer, this will be a terrace full of café tables.

The restaurant is at first floor level. The glass rooflight runs the length of the structure; even on the dullest day the light is inspiring. At one end, there's a stainless steel bar; at the other there's a crustacea bar. The furniture is evocative of the period of the original building, with chairs dressed in car leather and chrome, and petrol-blue banquettes. Naturally, customers who book a table in the restaurant will expect a fine meal, as well as exciting surroundings. Executive chef is Andrew Sargent, responsible for alle four kitchens at the Gastrodrome. He was previously a chef for King Hussein of Jordan. His cuisine is influenced by French and Italian styles. Popular signature dishes are wood-roasted crustacea, hot lobster with caviar butter and roast salmon with tomato, red onion and coriander.

Make sure you set aside a good couple of hours to investigate all the fascinating parts that make up the Bluebird Gastrodrome. As Terence Conran said; "It's my abiding principle that if people are offered something well made, well designed and of decent quality, at a price they can afford, then they will like it - and buy it." Myself, I came away laden… and already planning my next visit.

LITTLE ITALY

Across all of Soho, there's a buzz of excitement. Open-topped convertibles in flame-red or deep-shining black crawl ostentatiously across intersections, Soho's pedal rickshaws skim stealthily by, adding another colourful touch to the exotic eastern flavour of the area. Walking down Frith Street towards Chinatown, through the heart of Soho, you'll come across a particular restaurant on your left that looks neither very big nor particularly chic, but there'll be a knot of people at the door waiting to be beckoned through its doors and a throng of diners inside obviously having a high time.

Little Italy is a restaurant without pretensions, whose reputation had been built on its excellent food; but it's small, so I suggest if you would like to eat Italian in the West End that you ensure a table for yourself by booking well ahead. Saturday evenings in the summertime, of course, are particularly busy. There is a street level café-bar which is a perfect place to sip the excellent coffee and watch the crowds, and at the rear, there are two smart split level dining rooms. The atmosphere is relaxed, coolly metropolitan, with menus to match.

I was lucky enough to find a table and I was greatly impressed by the friendly attitude of the extremely busy staff. It took me a while to choose: there were some wonderful pasta dishes on the menu, and the specials of the day sounded tempting. However, I decided to start with an antipasto of char-grilled vegetables, seasoned with balsamic vinegar and extra virgin olive oil. It arrived speedily, considering the crush, and was delicious. My main course was *saltimbocca alla Romana* - pan-fried veal topped with Parma ham and fresh sage in a white wine sauce. It was extremely good, the different flavours harmoniously blending together, the veal succulent. My side dish, a rocket salad with Parmesan shavings, was fresh and nutty. I concluded with a simple vanilla sorbet, and then treated myself to an espresso and a shot of grappa Alexander 1997, to send me off with courage into the late-night crowds. Just up the street from Little Italy is Ronnie Scott's, without a doubt the country's premier jazz club, showcase for a succession of famous names. Little Italy, certainly, is an honourable neighbour and a great place for a pre-theatre meal, a short and fascinating stroll from all the West End theatres. To be recommended for its wonderfully engaging atmosphere, with smiling, helpful staff and its wonderful cuisine that is a harmonious combination of the traditional and the innovative.

BENTLEY'S SEAFOOD RESTAURANT AND OYSTER BAR

Although much has changed on the London restaurant scene, it is one of the city's paradoxical charms that the old and time-tested continues to find an honoured place amongst so much that is seductively up-to-the-minute. The art of it is to cleverly combine the best of the classical and traditional with the brightest trends and developing tastes of the day.

One such landmark establishment is Bentley's Restaurant and Oyster Bar in West End's Swallow Street. It has specialised in the finest of fish, seafood and oysters since 1916 and its menu, overseen by talented head chef Jamie Kimm, features good old-fashioned fish and chips and various classic oyster dishes alongside adventurous new flavours such as seared tuna, halibut *brandade* and gnocchi of crayfish.

First established by William Bentley, the restaurant passed to his three sons, Bill, Derek and Roy. Under their steward-ship it flourished and expanded, until it was eventually sold to outside buyers in 1976. It has since been much revamped and revitalized and is a favourite with today's celebrities and politicians, who can take advantage of its private dining-room facility and its discreet and romantic two-person 'Royal Box' in the Oyster Bar, which if desired can be closed off from the rest of the bar.

The everyday running of Bentley's is in the capable hands of multi-lingual Brussels-born Managing Director Giuseppe Dewilde. He says: "I want to carry Bentley's through into the Millennium. Changes to the menu will occur, of course, but we will vigorously retain all of its traditional values of excellent service and fine food."

We visited one Saturday lunchtime, and admired the impressive Oyster Bar: a long wooden bar with high stools and towels at the ready for oyster lovers to wipe their hands on. On weekdays, this part of the restaurant is especially popular. We were shown a lovely quiet table and were looked after with skill and great friendliness by Khalid.

After sharing a plate of scintillating Donegal oysters, I chose a delightful dish of roast skate with gratin of macaroni, wild mushrooms and artichokes, accompanied by vegetables *du jour*. My companion was equally happy with her gnocchi of crayfish, also with wild mushrooms and an oil of basil. We left the choice of accompanying wine to Khalid, who suggested a superlative Chablis 1998 Grand Regnard, a 100% Chardonnay.

We completed an unforgettable meal with jasmin and vanilla *crème brûlée* and a *tarte aux pommes* with Calvados. Located down a quiet and shady alley just off busy Regent Street, Bentley's is a companionable refuge from the turmoil of London. Seek it out like a treasure… you will not be disappointed.

L'ESCARGOT

Greek Street is in the very heart of lively, cosmopolitan Soho, as full of life by day as it is by night. Michelin-starred L'Escargot, one of London's most celebrated restaurants, has had its home here since the 1920s and is as stylish and popular today as it was back then. At lunchtime, the clientele are mostly drawn from the local business community and L'Escargot offers them an excellent short three-menu package that includes an aperitif, a starter, main course, pudding, 1/3 of a bottle of very good house wine, with fresh flowers and place cards on the table, representing good value for £45 per person.

In the evening, patrons are likely to be heading for the theatre, or to have come from there… the West End theatres are only a short walk away and L'Escargot provides large and small groups with elegant and exclusive spaces, like the Picasso Room and the unusual and interesting Barrel Vault Room.

The furnishings include comfortable red leather chairs and there are original paintings on the wall by world-famous artists like Miró, Chagall, Léger and Picasso.

The à la carte menu is prodigious. I didn't find it easy to choose from amongst so many tasty-sounding dishes. Eventually I settled for a carpaccio of seabass and salmon, lemon dressing and wild roquette, followed by a main dish of succulent Black Angus rib eye steak, fondant potato, confit of garlic and shallots and wild mushrooms. I concluded a wonderful meal with a delicious pear and almond tart with clotted cream and a cup of Costa Rican coffee.

CARLUCCIOS

Antonio Carluccio is internationally known from his television shows. He is obviously a man who enjoys life, with a gleam in his eyes and sunshine in his voice. His restaurant-cum-delicatessen in London's trendy Neal Street is just one of his many projects. He has written several cookery books, the latest of which, 'Antonio Carluccio's Vegetables' contains 200 recipes with 40 different vegetables. "We Italians take our vegetables seriously," Carluccio says. And that

becomes evident when you dine in the tasteful restaurant simply called Carluccio's. Antonio Carluccio became involved in the restaurant world almost by coincidence. 19 years ago, he came to England - "for a woman", he laughs. "I have never been a chef, I am a passionate cook. A chef is someone who cooks in a restaurant, and I have always cooked at home, for myself, and for friends. It all started when I entered a Sunday Times contest in 1980. I was a wine

merchant at the time, but during that period I also started to manage this restaurant, which was owned by my brother-in-law Terence Conran. I am responsible for the food and the style - but I don't do administration."

Everything that comes from Carluccio's kitchen is purely Italian: traditional, simple, prepared with the very best ingredients, used in such a way that their original flavour is subtly enhanced.

Italy is a culinary gold mine, with some 10,000 original recipes of their own. There are 20 different areas, each with their own language, habits, and food. Carluccio finds it important that each area maintains its individuality and its traditional dishes, which should be prepared to perfection.

"Italian cuisine is very simple, and that simplicity is its best quality. Only the best ingredients are good enough: the finest olive oil, the most fragrant truffles, tomatoes with real flavour."

Carluccio has made it his mission to show the world that Italian food is more than lasagne and spaghetti. It earned him the 'Commendatore' from the Italian government, a high distinction of which he is extremely proud.

The cosy, pleasant restaurant in Neal Street can seat some 70 guests. The menu offers the chef's own favourites: risotto, pasta, polenta - and vegetables, of course. Fresh salads, seemingly simple pastas that taste exquisite, classic desserts, per-

fect coffee. Carluccio's favourite ingredient, white truffle, is imported fresh and is used with great care - not surprising, considering that this rare delicacy costs some £ 2,500 per kilo. "You really eat the scent of a white truffle," he says. His delicatessen next door sells all sorts of Italian ingredients and dishes. And recently, he opened his first Carluccio's café-delicatessen, where you can eat the finest simple Italian food for a modest price. In the next five years, he want to open 30 more, four of which will be in London. Antonio Carluccio obviously wants to share his love for fine Italian food with as many people as possible.

CLARKE'S

As soon as you step into this lovely Notting Hill restaurant, you know you've arrived somewhere rather special. The bright, fresh atmosphere seems to envelop you, draw you into its warm, affectionate ambience. There are many who will assure you that Sally Clarke's is their favourite London restaurant; quite something, considering the number of excellent ones there are around. Beneath your feet are glowing wooden floors and on the understated pale walls, contemporary paintings by such luminaries as Joe Tilsm and Howard Hodgkin catch the eye. You descend the staircase to the 70 to 80-seat dining area and are at once beguiled by the drama of the open-plan kitchen, overseen by Sally herself.

Each day, Sally devises her own four-course set menu that skilfully balances one dish with the next. Customers are more than content to allow Sally's genius to lead the way through their meal, from entrée to the coffee and chocolate truffles. At the time of writing, the full four-course meal costs £ 44 - and I can assure you it is good value - without your wine, of which there is a generous and well-informed choice.

Sally Clarke spent five years working for celebrated Michael's Restaurant, in Santa Monica, California, before returning to open her London restaurant, and she brings a refreshing American touch to her classic English cuisine. Grilling is quite frequently the preferred method of cooking. Healthy eating is essential to her cuisine, it is her philosophy and her passion. She is absolutely insistent on procuring the very freshest of seasonal vegetables, herbs and fruit and whenever possible they will be organic. At Clarke's, you will find no heavy sauces… everything is kept simple and straightforward, allowing the real and exhilarating tastes to emerge. I have to admit I had almost forgotten how delicious a carrot could be!

Immediately next door to Clarke's is Sally's own shop, where you can purchase almost everything used in the restaurant: organic vegetables, fine herbs, wonderfully tasty Italian olive oils, choice fruits, good American wines, home-made French conserves, bouquets of flowers… and bread. Sally has her own wholesale bakery that provides the shop, as well as many top-class hotels and restaurants, with a superb range of quality breads: American sourdough, 100% rye, sun-dried tomato bread, oatmeal and a seductive wholeweat and honey loaf that is unforgettable.

It you've enjoyed your meal at Clarke's, you may wish to try your hand at recreating Sally's dishes. Before you leave you can ask for Sally Clarke's new book: Recipes from Her Restaurant, Shop and Bakery. With that, and your purchases from the shop, you can bring some of Sally's magic into your own kitchen.

BIBENDUM

Terence Conran has transformed the London restaurant scene almost single-handedly and the list of restaurants and hotels with which he is associated is a long one indeed. His purchase of the ageing headquarters of the famous Michelin tyre company predates many of his more recent make-overs and its immediate success in the 1980s perhaps gave him the courage to invest in developments on other sites he has discovered.

It took over two years to plan and execute the fundamental changes to the vacant tyre factory, but today the site on Fulham Road is a stylish and modern combination of functionalism and affluence. The restaurant, Bibendum, shares the space with a bar, a downstairs Oyster Bar and a flourishing retail outlet.

Everyone would recognise the corpulent figure of the Michelin man, but I, for one, had no idea this stout and cheerful figure, right from his birth back in 1898, possessed a name… Bibendum. Although his image appears in various guises throughout the restaurant and bar, eating at Bibendum will not, thankfully, bestow the Michelin man's generous proportions upon patrons. The food, prepared under the overall guidance of head chef Matthew Harris, is classic French, an invigorating mix of Parisian brasserie and chic Mediterranean, relying on the highest quality meat, fish and seafood and supremely fresh seasonal vegetables. The accompanying wine list, expertly chosen by Matthew Jukes, is extensive and encompasses every well-known wine region. Downstairs from Bibendum is the popular Bibendum Oyster Bar, a lovely and informal setting offering the choicest of oysters, caviar and seafood, supplementend by excellent salads, and complemented by a selection of appropriate wines which won't hurt your wallet.

A tall, square-nosed French *camion* is parked in what originally was the tyre-fitting bay. It sells a large selection of fresh seafood - lobster, crab, oysters, smoked salmon, caviar and all sorts of unusual varieties of fresh fish. Customers can buy straight from the van, or they can phone in their orders or place them on the internet. House delivery in central London is available.

Bibendum makes a convenient lunchtime stopover for shoppers in fashionable Fulham Road, and can be wholeheartedly recommended as a great destination in itself in the evening.

BANK

Within just six weeks of opening in 1996, Bank Restaurant and Bar was awarded the coveted Restaurant of the Year by the Times and has since won many other accolades, including Best Modern British Restaurant at the Carlton Food Awards in 1998. Reviews of the restaurant are consistently praiseworthy and Bank, very close to another modern icon, the hotel One Aldwych, is always very popular and much respected. Over the past few years, quite a few Victorian and Edwardian banks have been converted into restaurants, but this one is especially beautiful. A huge space accommodating up to 300 diners, a state of the art open kitchen and immaculate attention to detail make Bank

ingredients, a typical meal might start with roast baby aubergines, bocconcini and pesto. Continue with roast salmon with shallots, olives and caper compote, with a cream of fennel and conclude with a delightful cappuccino mousse. But the choice is immense and an enjoyment in itself, so take your time! The chic wine list, too, will provide you with yet further diversion.

Fish and crustacea are Bank's special strengths, and the restaurant obtains its wonderfully fresh supply from Cutty's, London's premier fish merchants.

The very modern interior of Bank is spectacular to a degree - look up and you'll see a huge 20-tonne glass sculpture sus-

an experience to be savoured. Its position, perfectly placed to draw patrons from the City, from Covent Garden and the West End, is a factor in its success, but without its enviable reputation for fine cuisine this, of course, would hardly matter. The menu has been devised by Michelin-starred chef Christian Delteil and Bank Group Chairman and co-founder Tony Allan, himself a head chef by the tender age of 20 and trained at two of the capital's most celebrated hotels, the Dorchester and Claridge's. Using the freshest possible of

pended (yes, very securely!) from the ceiling and snaking across the entire restaurant. Design was in the hands of Julian Wickham, whose work can also be experienced at Harvey Nichols' Fifth Floor Restaurant and at Kensington Place.

Unusually, you can walk into Bank between 7.30 and 10.30 every weekday morning and sit down to a classic full English breakfast. This could include scrambled eggs with smoked salmon, or with haddock, or how about a not-so-traditional helping of beluga caviar with potato waffles and creme fraiche?

The bar at Bank is a popular destination in itself with the youthful crowd of successful media people, who come for the long list of celebrated cocktails the bar staff prepare with theatrical skill and good humour. The names of the drinks run from the traditional rum punch and margarita through to more unusual combinations like Razzberreto, June Bug… and Zombie, a killer featuring dark rum, light rum, lime juice, orange and apricot liqueur and orange and pineapple juice. Whatever you choose to eat or drink, you can bank on Bank for an evening out you won't easily forget.

MIRABELLE

I once asked a famous Michelin-starred chef who, according to him, was the greatest culinary master in London. Without hesitation, he answered: Marco Pierre White. It is no coincidence that White is the only British chef who has been awarded three Michelin stars. After a relatively modest start at Harvey's, south of the River Thames, his career took off with a vengeance and nowadays, his name is connected with various great restaurants in London. One of those is Mirabelle in Curzon Street, a one-star restaurant with a splendid past.

In the 1950's and 60's Mirabelle was one of the smartest gastronomic addresses in London, where royals and film stars came to enjoy the finest cuisine. But just like some of the stars from that era, Mirabelle slowly lost its glamour. Until 1998, that is, when it re-opened its doors, more stylish and wonderful than ever. Since then, Mirabelle has won numerous awards, not only for its splendid cuisine and its excellent wine list, but also for its wonderful decor. The simple lobby and the elegant bar are decorated in classic 30's style. The restaurant itself is stunning: a highly polished parquet floor, tables laid with crisp white linen and sparkling glasses. The menu boasts British classics,

such as calf's liver with bacon and sage in an onion gravy or potted shrimps, as well as simple French dishes, such as *choucroute alsacienne*.

To enjoy the one-star cuisine here, you don't need to be a millionaire: the set lunch of the day costs a modest £ 14.95 for one course, while the three-course version will set you back no more than £ 17.95.

The wine list features excellent wines which would push up the final bill, but there are also more reasonable, very nice wines.

Besides the main restaurant, Mirabelle also has two private dining rooms: the Pine Room, a beautiful, classic room with a floor in dark red leather; and the Chinese Room, with its refined decor and breath-takingly beautiful hand-painted wallpaper in silver and jade.

I chose one of Marco Pierre White's signature dishes: *foie gras parfait en gelée,* followed by *daube à l'ancienne,* a classic French stew made with the best Aberdeen Angus. The *tarte sablé* of dark chocolate was the perfect ending to a perfect meal.

While I sipped a cup of delicious coffee, I decided to come back one day for Sunday brunch - it is supposed to be a feast of typically British dishes, prepared with the utmost French *finesse.*

ASSAGGI

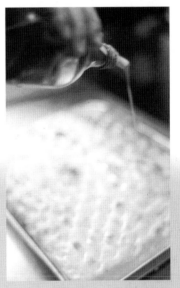

To find this small but delectable Italian restaurant, it might be easier to look for the Chepstow Arms, in Chepstow Road, Notting Hill, first… for Assaggi is immediately above the pub, reached by a brightly-painted entrance hall and stairs. There are just 12 tables in the restaurant, set about on wooden boards under a high ceiling. Competition for them is great, because the reputation of Assaggi, a favourite of many media figures, has spread far and wide. And with some reason. The cuisine is unpretentious and full of wonderful flavours.

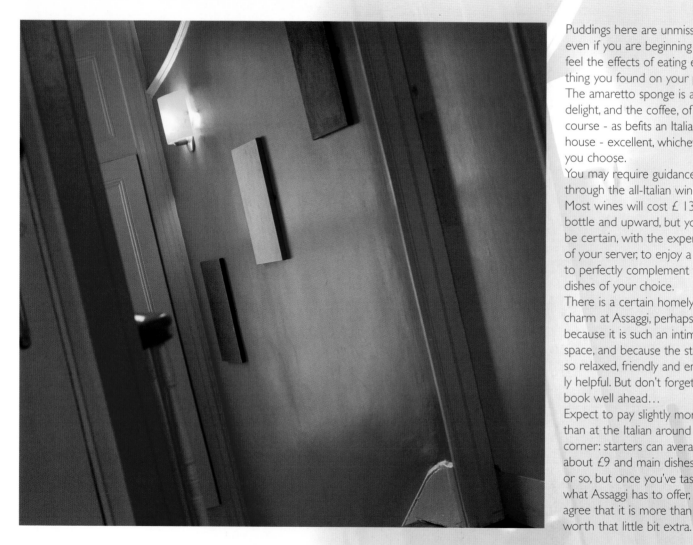

Puddings here are unmissable - even if you are beginning to feel the effects of eating everything you found on your plate. The amaretto sponge is a delight, and the coffee, of course - as befits an Italian house - excellent, whichever you choose.

You may require guidance through the all-Italian wine list. Most wines will cost £13 a bottle and upward, but you can be certain, with the expertise of your server, to enjoy a wine to perfectly complement the dishes of your choice.

There is a certain homely charm at Assaggi, perhaps because it is such an intimate space, and because the staff are so relaxed, friendly and endlessly helpful. But don't forget to book well ahead…

Expect to pay slightly more than at the Italian around the corner: starters can average about £9 and main dishes £18 or so, but once you've tasted what Assaggi has to offer, you'll agree that it is more than worth that little bit extra.

There's an extensive choice of mouth-watering starters. Even if you choose a simple chicken soup, you will find it less plain than you might have expected, with an added splash of red wine and a filling of spiced lamb tortelloni.

Fish is always popular at Assaggi, because it is prepared with a skill bordering on the uncanny. My particular favourite, monkfish, will come in delicate fingers, wrapped like a valuable gift in thin wafers of pancetta. The supremely fresh seasonal vegetables are a delight, too - even the humble potato is transformed into a delicacy.

199

USEFUL INFORMATION

HOTELS

COVENT GARDEN HOTEL p 8
10, Monmouth Street
London W1Y 4LB
Ph. (0044) (0) 171/ 806 10 00
Fax (0044) (0) 171/ 806 11 00
e-Mail : covent@firmdale.com
website : www.firmdale.com
Location : Covent Garden

THE METROPOLITAN p 12
19, Old Park Lane
London W1Y 4LB
Ph. (0044) (0) 171/ 447 10 20
Fax (0044) (0) 171/ 447 10 22
e-Mail : res@metropolitan.co.uk
website : www.metropolitan.co.uk
Location : Mayfair

THE CONNAUGHT p 18
Carlos Place, Mayfair
London W1Y 6AL
Ph. (0044) (0) 171/ 499 70 70
Fax (0044) (0) 171/ 495 32 62
e-Mail : info@the-connaught.co.uk
website :http://www.savoy-group.co.uk
Location : Mayfair

SYDNEY HOUSE p 22
9-11 Sydney Street, Chelsea
London SW3 6PU
Ph. (0044) (0) 171/ 376 77 11
Fax (0044) (0) 171/ 376 42 33
e-Mail : sydneyhousehotel@see-london.com
website : www.sydneyhousehotel.com
Location : Chelsea

THE HALKIN p 28
Halkin Street, Belgravia
London SW1X 7DJ
Ph. (0044) (0) 171/ 333 10 00
Fax (0044) (0) 171/ 333 12 11
e-Mail : sales@halkin.co.uk
website : www.halkin.co.uk
Location : Belgravia

NUMBER ELEVEN CADOGAN GARDENS p 32
11, Cadogan Gardens, Sloane Square
London SW3 2RJ
Ph. (0044) (0) 20 7730 7000
Fax (0044) (0) 20 7730 5217
e-Mail : reservations@number-eleven.co.uk
Website : www.number-eleven.co.uk
Location : Chelsea

FOUNTAINS SUITES p 36
1, Lancaster Terrace
Hyde Park
London W2 3PF
Ph. (0044) (0) 20 7706 7070
Fax (0044) (0) 20 7706 7006
e-Mail : sales@living-rooms.co.uk
website : www.living-rooms.co.uk
Location : Hyde Park/ Bayswater

N° 5 MADDOX STREET p 39
5, Maddox Street, Mayfair
London W1R 9LE
Ph. (0044) (0) 20 7647 0200
Fax (0044) (0) 20 7647 0300
e-Mail : no5maddoxst@living-rooms.co.uk
website : www.living-rooms.co.uk
Location : Mayfair

THE HALCYON p 42
81, Holland Park
London W11 3RZ
Ph. (0044) (0) 171/ 727 72 88
Fax (0044) (0) 171/ 229 85 16
e-Mail : sales.halcyon@virgin.net
website : halcyon-hotel.co.uk
Location : Holland Park/ Kensington

MYHOTEL BLOOMSBURY p 46
11-13, Bayley Street, Bloomsbury
London WC1 B3HD
Ph. (0044) (0) 20 7667 600
Fax (0044) (0) 20 7667 600
e-Mail : guest-services@myhotels.co.uk
website : www.myhotels.co.uk
Location : Bloomsbury

THE CLIVEDEN TOWN HOUSE p 50
24-26 Cadogan Gardens
London SW3 2RP
Ph. (0044) (0) 171/ 730 64 66
Fax (0044) (0) 171/ 730 02 36
e-Mail : reservations@clivedentownhouse.co.uk
website : www.clivedentownhouse.co.uk
Location : Chelsea

ONE ALDWYCH p 54
One Aldwych
London WC2B 4BZ
Ph. (0044) (0) 20 300 1000
Fax (0044) (0) 20 300 1001
e-Mail : sales@onealdwych.co.uk
website : www.onealdwych.co.uk
Location : Strand/ Covent Garden

THE PORTOBELLO HOTEL p 60

22, Stanley Gardens
London W11 2NG
Ph. (0044) (0) 20/ 7727 2777
Fax (0044) (0) 20/ 7792 9641
e-Mail : info@portobello-hotel.co.uk
website : www.portobello-hotel.co.uk
Location : North Kensington

THE ROOKERY p 64

Peter's Lane
Cowcross Street
London EC1M 6DS
Ph. (0044) (0) 20 7336 0931
Fax (0044) (0) 20 7336 0932
e-Mail : reservations@rookeryhotel.co.uk
website : www.rookeryhotel.com
Location : East London/ Liverpool Street
Station

ST. MARTINS LANE p 68

St. Martins Lane
London WC2N 4HX
Ph. (0044) (0) 171/ 300 55 00
Fax (0044) (0) 171/ 300 55 01
e-Mail : stmartinslane@compuserve.com
Location : Covent Garden

THE MILESTONE HOTEL & APARTMENTS p 76

Kensington Court
London W8 5DL
Ph. (0044) (0) 20 7917 1000
Fax (0044) (0) 20 7917 1010
e-Mail : guestservices@milestone.redcarna-
tionhotels.com
website : www.redcarnationhotels.com
Location : Kensington

GREAT EASTERN HOTEL p 82

Liverpool Street
London EC2M 7 QN
Ph. (0044) (0) 20 7618 5000
Fax (0044) (0) 207 618 5001
e-Mail : restaurantres@great-eastern-
hotel.co.uk
Location : East London/ Liverpool Street
Station

SANDERSON p 88

50, Berners Street
London W1P 4AD
Ph. (0044) (0) 207 300 1400
Fax (0044) (0) 207 300 1401
e-Mail : sanderson.isuk@virginnet.co.uk
Location : Soho/ Oxford Street

RESTAURANTS

THE NEW VEERASWAMY RESTAURANT p 94

Victory House
101, Regent Street
London W1R 8RS
Ph. (0044) (0) 20 7734 1401
Fax (0044) (0) 20 7439 8434
e-Mail : action@realindianfood.com
Website : www.realindianfood.com
Location : Mayfair

QUO VADIS p 98

26-29 Dean Street
London W1A 6LL
Ph. (0044) (0) 171/ 437 95 85
Fax (0044) (0) 171/ 434 99 72
Website : www.whitestarline-org.uk
Location : Soho

THE GASTRODROME/ CANTINA DEL PONTE p 102

The Butlers Wharf Building
36, Shad Tames
London SE1 2YE
Ph. (0044) (0) 171/ 403 54 03
Fax (0044) (0) 171/ 403 02 67
website : www.conran.com
Location : Southwark

THE GASTRODROME/ BLUE PRINT CAFÉ p 102

The Butlers Wharf Building
36, Shad Tames
London SE1 2YE
Ph. (0044) (0) 171/ 378 70 31
Fax (0044) (0) 171/ 357 88 10
website : www.conran.com
Location : Southwark